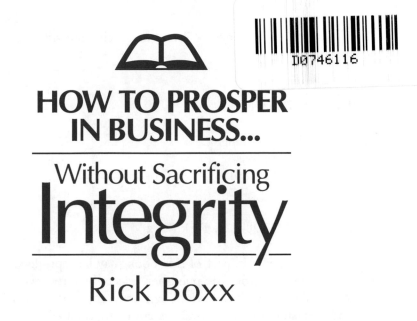

HOW TO PROSPER IN BUSINESS...

Without Sacrificing
Integrity

Rick Boxx

How to Prosper in Business Without Sacrificing Integrity

Rick Boxx

ISBN 1-929478-53-4

Cross Training Publishing
317 West Second Street
Grand Island, NE 68801
(308) 384-5762

Library of Congress Cataloging in Publication Data in Progress.

CONTENTS

INTRODUCTION

Would you sell your integrity for $1 million? $10 million? $100 million? Many people in business everyday sell their soul for a lot less than any of these amounts. If you have a price in mind, you are in trouble.

If profits mean more to you than your reputation, then it is time for self-examination. Business leaders often times get so focused on succeeding in business that they do not see the brokenness they have left scattered along the path. There is an almost daily tension in business: profits or integrity?

Profits can give temporary satisfaction, while integrity is longer lasting. This book was written to assist business leaders in their journey towards prosperity, *with* their integrity remaining intact. This approach begs the question, what if you have to choose between profits and integrity?

To answer that question we will turn to the best selling business resource ever: The Holy Bible. In Part I of this book we will lay a solid foundation for your business by recognizing our obligation to our Maker to put Him first. We will also examine the key attributes of a business with integrity. Some attributes like excellence, accountability, and recognizing that we have a mission greater than profits will be explored in more depth in the subsequent chapters.

In Part II we will examine management skills like planning, becoming a servant leader, and developing our greatest asset, our people. After the solid foundation is laid we will turn to the final section of this time tested business model, finances. Practical approaches to generous giving, managing your money, and eliminating debt await you in this section. Finally we will discuss how you continue putting God first in your business during the most trying time in business, prosperity.

In the end you will have to make the choice. Do I use the practical tools in this book to make more money, but ignore the call to walk with integrity, or do I trust God's Word when He gave Joshua the answer to this timeless dilemma in Joshua 1:8, "Do not let this Book of the Law depart from your mouth; meditate on it day and night, so that you may be careful to do everything written in it. Then you will be prosperous and successful?"

God has a plan for your business. God's plan is a plan designed to prosper you *without* sacrificing integrity. Wouldn't it be much easier to work with God towards the goals that He has in mind, rather than to work against God? In this book we will embark on a journey, seeking God's direction for your business. His plan is the perfect plan for your business. Can your plan possibly improve on the Master's? Whose plan do you wish to follow?

It is your choice to make, but someday you will have an opportunity to stand before God Almighty, and find out the eternal consequences of your choice. I hope you hear, "Well done, good and faithful servant."

ACKNOWLEDGEMENTS

The journey that birthed this book has been long and tedious. Many people deserve to be recognized for their role in this project, and to each of them I am thankful.

I am most grateful to my Lord and Savior. He has encouraged me when I have been frustrated. He has pushed me when I have been slothful, and He has loved me when I have been unlovable. Thank you, Lord, for your patience.

Special thanks to David Thompson, Wil and Tracy Turner and my CBMC Forum group for their faithful encouragement and support. I also want to thank Susan Titus Osborn for her editing talents, and that red ink pen she must have surely exhausted on my first draft. Gary Ascanio has been a tremendous prayer warrior, and encourager, over the years whom I will never forget. To Gregg Motley, my first partner in business, I will be eternally grateful for his impact on my life in so many ways, but especially for many of the insightful principles he shared with me, which have been woven throughout this book.

My board of directors faithfully stood by me over the years, cajoling and encouraging me to continue moving forward. Thanks guys! Many people have helped me work on the manuscript at various stages, like Ann and Wayne Pilkinton, my mother-in-law Nancy Taral, my sister-in-law Judy Honigfort, Amy Sazama, Jack Houghton, Gordon Thiessen and probably others I have forgotten. To each of you I am very grateful.

Most importantly I want to thank my wife, Kathy. She has been there through the ups and downs, always faithful to love me and prod me into action. She is my helpmate, my editor, my encourager, and most of all, my friend. Thank you Kathy for your loving faithfulness.

Part I: Leadership Principles

Putting God First

"The earth is the Lord's, and everything in it, the world,
and all who live in it." Psalm 24:1

Building a prosperous business requires a solid foundation. This was never so apparent as when the world watched Enron, one of the most esteemed companies of the 1990's, crumble into bankruptcy in 2002. As investigators and auditors picked through the ruble they found that the foundation of this company was nothing more substantial than sand.

Not only did this very profitable company disintegrate, it did it almost overnight. Along with the demise of this company, thousands of its employees were left unemployed, and the reputation of several executives was ruined. What could cause a huge, respected business to fail so quickly? According to many news accounts, the answer is a pervasive lack of integrity.

If Enron had been the only major failure due to issues of character, it would be easy to dismiss the problem as simply being a small group of greedy people duping the public. Instead, we have witnessed WorldCom, Global Crossing, Tyco, choosing money over integrity and the list goes on and on. This demands a closer look for the underlying cause.

Upon close examination I believe you will find the problem rooted in the worldview of our business culture. When people make decisions, like whether or not to hide debts or losses, they filter their thought process through their belief system, or what's often referred to as their worldview.

The predominant worldview relating to business ethics is founded on "moral relativism." In layman's terms, there are no *absolute* right or wrong decisions, everything is relative. This means it is okay to cook the books, or use a conflict of interest for your personal gain, without being concerned about the resulting impact on others. After all, your corporate ethics department would have likely told you to use your best judgment, because your decision is relative to what *you* think is right or wrong.

Although we do not have time in this book to dive deeper into this subject, the important thing to remember is that moral relativism is founded on the belief that we are not beholden to a God, or his rules.

Imagine stepping out of a plane flying at 20,000 feet and saying to yourself, 'I am not going to fall, because the law of gravity does not apply to me.' After falling 19,000 feet I am confident you would be a firm believer in the law of gravity. Just as God designed the law of gravity, He also developed guidelines for our life. Guidelines like thou shalt not kill, or thou shalt not steal are just as absolute as the law of gravity, and they also have consequences if disobeyed, eternal consequences.

Studies consistently show that a majority of the population now believes that there are no absolute right or wrongs, but yet these same people claim they believe in God. If there is a God, and He has consistently communicated His laws over thousands of years to dozens of authors, why do we not think they apply to us?

As we discussed previously, a prosperous business with integrity requires a solid foundation. The foundation this book prescribes is obeying God's commands and principles as communicated in the Holy Bible. The only worldview that has proven successful for thousands of years is God's way.

Why Put God First?

Trying to manage a business without putting God first makes as much sense as playing in a Super Bowl game without a coach. The football coach recruits the team, designs the playbook, calls the plays, and leads the team to victory after victory. Imagine playing the biggest game ever and leaving the coach at home. As ridiculous as that seems it is more reasonable than leaving God out of our business affairs.

God brought us into this world, He gave us a playbook called the Bible, He calls the plays in our lives, through circumstances and His Holy Spirit, and He gives us victory after victory in our lives. He is like a football coach to us. Yet, everyday in millions of businesses God is left at home. What a tragedy!

God not only has the needed wisdom to make our business more profitable, He is truth. To prosper *and* maintain integrity requires strict adherence to a code of ethics. God authored the original code of ethics. His truths have guided leaders for thousands of years, into and through successful ventures. When these leaders also obeyed God's commands and principles their ventures reflected integrity.

Some of us will someday own or manage our own businesses. Some will work for others. Either way, God wants to lead our team. After all God was Solomon's coach, and he went on to become the wealthiest man on earth. If God can handle the tremendous challenges and complexities of a kingdom the size of Solomon's, He can certainly handle our problems.

As Dave waited outside Sam's office in the hot and misty dry-cleaning plant he overheard Sam's parting words to Mary.

"Mary, it grieves me to see all the troubles you have experienced since your husband died last fall. I sincerely want to help you any way that I can."

"Sam, you have been so generous. I will pay you back this $1,000 as soon as I can." Mary said with determination.

"No you won't." replied Sam "God has blessed me with the ability to help people like you. Catch up those utility bills, and go enjoy an evening with those precious grandchildren of yours with whatever is left."

After Mary had left the room Sam said, "I'm sorry, Dave, for the delay in our meeting."

"You really care about these people, don't you?" Dave asked with admiration.

"Yes, I do. Caring for Mary and my other employees is an example of my struggle with what to do with this business when I begin my missionary work in Peru."

"Are you planning on keeping the business or selling?" Dave asked.

"Dave, Sara and I have prayed long and hard about this business. We have decided that if *you* will manage it for us we will keep it."

"I am flattered that you would consider me so trustworthy, Sam, but I don't have any dry-cleaning experience. I've always been in retail clothing."

"You're a fast learner," exclaimed Sam, " and I have production people who are the best in the business. I need a manager who knows how to keep the customers happy, and one who will care for my staff."

"What are you willing to pay?" Dave asked.

Sam took a deep breath. "I am willing to pay you $100,000 a year."

"$100,000 a year!" Dave blurted. "That's double what I'm making now!"

"Now hold on, Dave, you haven't heard the conditions. You know my commitment to the poor. I will pay you $100,000 a year, only if you agree to give $10,000 a year to the local homeless mission, and you help any less fortunate people that approach you personally."

"You mean like Mary?" Dave asked.

"Yes, like Mary," Sam replied. "I know these are unique requests, Dave, but I want these conditions met from your salary, not from the business. Will you do it?"

Dave cleared his throat and said, "$10,000 is a lot of money for charity. Although, it still leaves me with more than what I'm making now, and it's a great opportunity."

"Terrific, then it's settled," said Sam as he reached out to shake Dave's hand.

A year later, in Peru, Sam received word of his father's death. His father also owned a dry-cleaning business back home. Sam desired to turn his inherited business over to Dave, too, but first he decided to go home for the funeral and to check on the business.

While at home Sam discovered that Dave declined a request from Sam's plant manager for help on funeral expenses, when his four-year-old boy tragically died of cancer. Also, a single mother of three who had worked for Sam for many years, was evicted from her apartment after Dave declined her request for some help on her back rent.

Sam felt like someone had punched him in the stomach when he heard the stories. People, whom he loved and cared for, had suffered, without him, or anyone else, to help. He went to Dave and asked if these stories were true.

Sheepishly Dave replied, "Yes, I can't be responsible for their money problems."

"What about the mission for the homeless, Dave?" Sam asked. "Did you honor your pledge to give them $10,000?"

"I meant to," stated Dave, "but Susan and I needed some money for the closing on our new house so we were only able to give $2,500."

Imagine that you are Sam. You've paid a handsome salary to this friend with only two requirements, both of which he has broken. Your passion is in the caring for others, not the profits he's generated. Would you trust him with the newly inherited business your father just left you?

God must ask Himself that type of question every day. This situation is real! It's going on daily across the United States. God has entrusted each one of His followers with possessions they are not worthy of receiving. He has asked us to give generously back to His kingdom, and to help the less fortunate. Recent surveys show that giving has been declining for many years, and on average we are giving 2.5 percent or less! As for helping the needy, the church has abdicated much of that responsibility to the government. It's amazing God trusts us with any prosperity. Like Sam, God's heart truly grieves over our disobedience.

Imagine having a son who just turned sixteen. You have two cars available for him to drive, a brand new Mercedes and an older Chevrolet. Which one will you let him drive? If you are like most fathers he will be driving the Chevrolet. Is it because you don't love him enough? Of course not. It's because you have not had a chance to see how responsible he is with the less valuable model. If he shows himself responsible you will likely let him move up to the Mercedes, but not until he is ready. God is the same way. He rewards the faithful and disciplines the reckless.

In 1981, at the age of twenty-five, I was reckless and invincible. I received my CPA certificate, owned rental property, and was growing a well-performing stock portfolio. My next goal was to become an entrepreneur. I figured that my CPA experience would give me the required skills to accomplish anything, even a faddish used car rental agency. After all, "Rent-A-Wreck" was successful in California, so why couldn't I make it work in Kansas City?

Little did I know that God had a plan for that business. His plan was *failure*. If I had asked Him, maybe He would have warned me, maybe not, but I do know one thing. He wanted me to ask! God wants to be first, not only in our lives, but in our businesses as well.

Why does God allow us to fail? In my case it was to teach me humility, and possibly to teach me to stick to familiar activities, not businesses I don't understand. It was also to experience the anxiety, fear, embarrassment, and financial strain of a business failure to enable me to empathize with the many people I would meet and counsel over the years.

From these illustrations let's summarize. Why should we put God first? First of all, everything with which we have been blessed belongs to God. If we are not faithful and obedient with what He has already provided then why should he give us more?

God can make or break your business. It's His choice. We may not like His choices at times, but He is a loving father who knows best. He desires for us to love Him with all our hearts, minds, and souls. At the same time He demands our obedience and our respect. It's from our obedience that God can allow us to prosper.

Secondly, God is the fountain of knowledge. Visualize your business experiencing tremendous financial difficulties. A close friend contacts Peter Drucker, one of the most respected business consultants of our day, on your behalf. Mr. Drucker agrees to come and help for free, but only if you personally call and invite him. Would you call? Of course you would. God made Peter Drucker. God's wisdom far exceeds Mr. Drucker's, and He is willing to assist your business for free, but He's waiting for your invitation.

Many business people will pay thousands of dollars for consultants without ever going to the source of all knowledge for the answers. We still need to seek counsel, but seek God first. There are many reasons for putting God first in our businesses. For me, I want to hear those words "Well done, good and faithful servant."

How to Put God First

1. Examine your checkbook.

You usually only have to look in two places to determine where your heart lies, your checkbook and your schedule. I recommend that you first examine your personal life in these areas, then your business. In your personal checkbook look at the size checks you write for house payments, car payments, vacations, etc. Now look at the size checks you write for kingdom work. If you are like most people it's a stark contrast. You may rationalize or dismiss this whole process as irrelevant. Is it really? Didn't Jesus say that where your treasure is there your heart is also?

Once you have examined your personal priorities, shift your focus to your business. Many businesses establish priorities for their cash that are not in line with God's. There are six key areas that give many businesses trouble in their effort to put God first financially.

1. Business giving. According to IRS data from business tax returns, charitable giving is typically less than 1.5% of the net income. If this number was broken down further we would probably find that very little of that amount goes towards Christian causes. In fact, much of it probably goes to organizations such as the United Way, who many times specifically avoids having religious organizations as beneficiaries of the giving.

This is in contrast to what God would expect from us if we were going to honor Him with our first fruits.

A better model would be R.G LeTourneau. Mr.

LeTourneau, according to a book called, "Mover of Men and Mountains," decided that God had blessed him enough. Instead of giving God 10% and living on 90% he did the opposite, and began giving God 90% and living on 10%. In spite of this generosity, Mr. LeTourneau still lived a very blessed lifestyle and accomplished tremendous work for the kingdom of God.

2. Employee pay. Many businesses claim to be run by Christians, and then proceed to pay their employees so poorly that their testimony is minimized. If God blessed you with employees then He has given you a stewardship responsibility similar to a father. Does your payroll register reflect a kind shepherd, or a harsh taskmaster?

3. Officer's compensation. Many business owners pride themselves in following the world's advice of paying themselves first. They experience financial rewards at the expense of their staff, suppliers, and lenders. Others will pay themselves so poorly that their own family suffers while customers and staff benefit excessively. Finding the right balance requires seeking God's wise counsel.

3. Bonuses and perks. Many businesses lavish extravagant perks on senior management while ignoring their responsibility to others. Country club memberships, season tickets, golf outings are all the last to be cut in many workplaces while God's work goes without proper support.

4. Capital expenditures. Many businesses get enamored with the latest and greatest technology. Farmers often fall into the trap of wanting to have the latest combine at the expense of bankrupting the business. Using a $100,000 plus piece of equipment only three to four weeks out of a year is typically not very cost effective, but the lure of keeping up with the neighbors can make for poor decisions.

5. Debt. Businesses have been fooled into believing that debt is necessary for a business to operate. Debt is always a presumption on the future. So many people have learned to trust more in their banker than in God that it has caused a great blight on the financial strength of our business community.

2. Examine your schedule.

Here's another test, add up how much time you spent last week praying about your business, evangelizing your work-force, or discipling the existing believers in your workplace. What about your staff's hours? Are you open on Sunday? Do you or others in your employ work on Sunday?

Even if you believe that the new covenant no longer requires us to honor the Sabbath, as an employer there are many more issues. First of all, one of the principles behind why God created the Sabbath was because he designed our bodies to work most effectively when we get a day off for rest and reflection. If you are ignoring this much needed rest you are ignoring God's wisdom and likely are less productive. You also may be causing your employees to stumble if they do not have the opportunity to worship on Sundays. If you are coming up short, do not bury yourself with guilt.

God does not want your guilt; He wants your time, treasure, and talent. God commanded us to "Love Him with all our hearts, all our minds, and all our souls." God is a loving and jealous God. He desires an intimate relationship with His children that can only grow when we spend time in prayer, Bible study, and worship. Commit to the Lord to do better. Ask God for help in developing your priorities around Him. He will lead you to a closer relationship. He is certainly worthy, considering all He has given us.

3. Establish Priorities

The Lord will work to change your heart towards His priorities and away from worldly priorities if you just ask Him.

Several years ago, I was struggling with making a difficult decision in business. As I prayed and journaled, I wrote down several inspired thoughts. Although I was looking for a specific answer, I believe God instead gave me a list of lifelong priorities to be my filter for decisions, rather than giving me a specific answer. The priorities were God, family, work, and then my local church. Now this may seem simple, but for each priority God revealed to me some specific ways to go about addressing those priorities.

Probably the most distinct thing I have learned from that list over time has been what it means to put God first. Often times I have viewed serving in a ministry capacity as meaning I was putting God first. Instead what God meant was to put Him first by spending time with Him in prayer and in His Word.

By substituting time in the ministry, for this desired time with God, I leaped over the rightful place my family was supposed to have in my life. Now in my case that didn't mean time, as much as it did money. I sacrificed my family constantly for the needs of the ministry. God would rather have me focus on my family's needs first, rather than having my wife feeling like the business was my mistress.

Pray and ask what God would have your priorities be, and what that model would look like on a daily basis. Remember the high value God places on the marriage covenant when determining how to allocate your schedule.

4. Build Accountability.

After you have examined your company checkbook, your schedule, and have properly established your priorities you still have too many opportunities to fail unless you develop accountability. Lack of accountability seems to be the common denominator when you see leaders who have fallen. Do not let that happen to you. Determine to surround yourself with people who care enough and know enough about you to keep you on track.

Looking for accountability partners who will challenge your behavior becomes critical in the lure of the business world. If you are married, start with your spouse. They have a vested interest in your success, usually know you better than anyone else, and will deliver the hard, but loving blows that no one else may be willing to deliver. Most business leaders who have called us for counsel have received counsel from their spouse, but ignored their advice. It is easy to dismiss the counsel they give with the rationalization that they just don't understand my business. This rationalization, however, many times turns out to be the pride that goes before a fall. So, if you say your spouse is your accountability partner remember to heed their advice.

In business it is helpful to also have other business people as accountability partners. This can be in the form of a board of directors, or you can join several Christian business organizations that serve that role. Fellowship of Companies for Christ and CBMC Forums are two such groups I have been involved with over the years. They provide a safe place for you to share your business and personal issues with other Christians who understand the trials of business. Look for ways to plug into an accountability group that will keep you focused on putting God first in your business.

Part of accountability needs to be driven by procedures and habits you create. If you are committed to serving God with your money there needs to be a mechanism in place to assure that you actually write a first fruits check, rather than waiting until you have paid the bills, and then deciding how much to give God. Make a commitment as to when, how, and how much you are committed to investing in God's work.

Another group that you should leverage to hold you accountable are your employees. If they know you are committed to being transparent in your faith then you will have more likelihood of success. Sometimes this means you need to have an open book model of business so that they know how you are really doing with your business finances. In other cases it's by letting them hear your desires on a regular basis and challenging them to confront you when they see you beginning to stumble. This may be a humbling approach for many, but it can be very effective.

If we desire to prosper in business, the most important thing is to humbly accept the fact that God owns everything, and it's His discretion as to what blessings He will give. If we are not faithful with little, it is unlikely he will bless us with much.

That means there is a higher calling for your business than simply profits. It is God's desire for you to seek his perfect will to uncover that purpose. Remember faithfulness is measured first with eternal treasures in mind rather than financial treasures. Pray that God will show the way in your business, and in your personal life, to put Him first. God is the ultimate coach. Don't try to manage a business without Him!

Walking with Integrity

"Fear God and keep his commandments, for this is the whole duty of man. For God will bring every deed into judgment, including every hidden thing, whether it is good or evil." Ecclesiastes 12:13-14

Integrity. We hear the word a great deal, but what does it really mean? It seems to have taken on an unclear meaning. Anyone can claim they walk with integrity, but how do we determine if they really do?

According to *The American Heritage® Dictionary of the English Language, Fourth Edition,* integrity means "Steadfast adherence to a strict moral or ethical code." But to whose values are we adhering? If asked, recent public high school graduates will likely say morals are relative, depending on the situation and the person. If it seems right to them at that moment, then it must be okay. This has resulted in situational ethics, or moral relativism. Moral relativism proclaims that whatever I determine to be right in the circumstance before me, must surely be the proper route to take. According to this approach there are no absolutes.

This has to be the most poorly written curriculum ever. Imagine no absolutes. This computer I'm typing on, maybe it's really a refrigerator! That homicide committed last night over a gambling debt, maybe in that case murder was okay. Rationalizing sin this way has become a favorite pastime. Sin comes from being self-centered, rather than God centered. Moral relativism drips of selfishness.

As a banker there were occasions when a borrower would try and bend the rules. We would have loan agreements with specific conditions to be met if they wanted us to continue loaning them money. If these covenants were violated we had the authority, and usually the ability, to put someone out of business. They had a choice to make, were they going to follow the bank's rules, or were they going to try and play by their rules and suffer the consequences.

That's the dilemma in our society today. Whose rules are we going to play by? Are we playing by man's rules or God's rules? Business leaders have a choice to make. They can walk with integrity, and please God, or follow conventional wisdom and please themselves.

Walking with integrity will not always be popular. Jesus certainly modeled that principle. Conventional wisdom claims we have to occasionally lie and cheat in business to prosper. *God proclaims* true prosperity comes out of walking with integrity. Peace of mind and respect will come with integrity. Conventional wisdom, however, may leave you confused, and with little self respect.

Chapter One stressed the first and most important leadership principle in obtaining prosperity: *God is in charge*. With God as our boss, the second leadership principle must be walking in obedience to God, walking with integrity.

What is Integrity?

As stated previously, integrity means a steadfast adherence to a moral set of values. The word itself comes from the Latin root "integra," which means wholeness or completeness. The nature of the word demands an adherence to the set of values in *all* parts of our lives. For this to occur it has to flow from the heart. Our motives are critical in determining whether we are walking with integrity holistically, or if we are putting on a good show for others.

The moral set of values, to a Christian, should include the Ten Commandments, God's other commands to us in Scripture, and principles from the Bible. These commands according to God's Word have been etched on our hearts.

Our motives, however, should come from our desire to please God. Our integrity therefore flows from our relationship with God. It is more about who we are in Christ, than what we do. *Walking* with integrity pulls the two facets together; both *being* a person of integrity, and adhering to God's standards for our life.

A 1998 survey of students featured in "Who's Who Among American High School Students" found that almost half the students said the biggest problem facing their generation today is a decline in social and moral values. These same students proved their claims when 80 percent of them admitted they cheated in school. This was the highest percentage in the twenty-nine-year history of the survey.

A *Wall Street Journal* article from the March 26, 1996 issue titled, "For Many Executives, Ethics Appear to Be a Write-Off," claims that 76 percent of graduate level business students were willing to commit fraud by misstating write-offs that cut into their companies' profits. This compared to 47 percent of top executives surveyed. Both numbers reflect the poor values in business.

Strict adherence to a moral set of values is where many people fall. Many may do what is right in public, and give the appearance of integrity, while in their hearts, and in their private actions, they act wickedly.

It's the little indiscretions that set us up for sliding into bigger mistakes. Rex tempted me with a little sin. My wife, Kathy, needed a newer van. We purchased a newer used model from Rex. Rex loves to make deals. If bending the rules is necessary to make a deal he is happy to accommodate. As he began to prepare the paperwork he leaned over and said, "I'll go ahead and write this up for $1,000 less on the bill of sale so you can save on sales tax."

"No, thank you." I replied.

"It's not a problem. I do it all the time," claimed Rex.

Not wanting to make a big deal out of it, I once again said, "No, thank you."

The next day as we were signing the final papers, Rex attempted one more time. "I really hate to see you pay all of that sales tax unnecessarily. Let me go ahead and lower the bill of sale. No one will ever know."

"Rex," I said firmly, "I will know, and I do not care to do business that way."

Opportunities to take short cuts are offered in life frequently. Jesus said it best when he said that if we are not faithful in the little things, how could God trust us with the big ones. Strict adherence to God's standards is the best way to stay on the road to righteousness, but what should we do when we fall?

If you think because you have made mistakes you can't be a person of integrity, then you don't understand the nature of our God. All through scripture God chose leaders who failed in some area or another. King David, the person He called a "man after God's heart" committed murder and adultery, but God forgave him and used him in remarkable ways.

The model for us is when you sin you should repent, and then brush yourself off and start walking with integrity again. After all if you were walking to a friends house and fell down you wouldn't quit. You would instead pick yourself up and carry on.

Many people rationalize that their small indiscretions are not hurting anyone else, but is that true? While in banking I once investigated a bank fraud perpetrated by a bank president. This banker's theft of over $40,000 all began quite innocently. He was short some money one week and decided to add an extra trip to his mileage report. He never intended to do it again, but soon it became a regular occurrence. The end result of this initial minor infraction led to jail time and the requirement that he make restitution. He actually had to have his daughters braces removed by the dentist in order to help pay the restitution. This man's indiscretion not only impacted his life, but also had profound and negative consequences to his family, and others.

Just as little things done without integrity can precede a big fall, inconsequential items done *with integrity* can lead to being a person of character. These basic ingredients that we weave into our daily life, become the defining nature of our character. Many character qualities could be emphasized to attain the elusive goal of walking with integrity, but there are five pillars of integrity in business, which the Bible consistently stresses, and many companies have proven helpful in developing a workplace with integrity.

These five pillars include fear of the Lord, honesty, trustworthiness, excellence, and a servant heart. These traits and others will be explored in more depth throughout this book, but let's take a look briefly at each one.

1. Fear of the Lord is the defining difference between secular integrity and Biblical integrity. You can find businesses that are honest and trustworthy, but few show any sign of fearing the Lord. This does not mean the kind of fear we typically consider. This kind of fear is more about awe and respect.

Many years ago in public accounting I had a client who was very secretive of his affairs and very antagonistic about his money. One day an IRS agent showed up at his office. At some point this person asked for more information than this cantankerous contractor wanted to share. He physically removed this agent from his office in a very inappropriate way. He did not show the proper respect to this person in authority. As you might expect the consequences were not too pleasant. The next day several IRS agents swarmed into his office, each of them packing pistols. That day they obtained the desired documents.

In our lives and in our business we should show the proper respect and awe for the power almighty God has over our life. This proper level of respect comes from the spiritual disciplines of spending time with God, studying the Word of God, prayer, and fasting, and results in humility, and in a servant attitude. Fearing God is critical for walking with integrity. The next four pillars flow from understanding the love of God. If you truly love God with your heart, mind, and soul you will desire to please Him with the following attributes.

2. Honesty. Proverbs 12:19 teaches, "Truthful lips endure forever, but a lying tongue lasts only a moment." This verse illustrates the lasting importance of honesty, but in a workplace this has proven consistently to be the highest desired quality of a leader by staff members.

If a leader is expected to steer the course of a business it requires the confidence of others to follow. Any deception or dishonesty will quickly undermine a leader's effectiveness. This is where even the smallest of details can cloud the perception of someone's honesty. For instance, if you promise someone they are going to get a promotion within the next year, and circumstances cause you to change your mind, to that person you have been dishonest, even if there were reasonable explanations.

3. Trustworthiness is the next pillar. Luke 16:11 states, "So if you have not been trustworthy in handling worldly wealth, who will trust you with true riches?" In business your staff, your board, your customers, your suppliers, and many others must believe you are trustworthy before they will consistently trust you with things of value. This applies not only to people trusting you, but also to proving your trustworthiness to God. Have you proven your trustworthiness in what He has entrusted unto you? If you place profits over people why would God grace you with even more staff to manage?

4. Excellence is a quality we need to see more of in Christian businesses. God has called us to be a light to the world, a shining example in all that we do, this includes in and through our businesses. In Ecclesiastes 10:10 Solomon teaches, "If the ax is dull and its edge unsharpened, more strength is needed but skill will bring success." We should look for leaders with skill and a heart for excellence, as well as look to personally model that kind of attribute. We can then comfortably serve kings unashamedly.

5. The fifth pillar of integrity is a servant heart. Ephesians 6:7-8 teaches, "Serve wholeheartedly, as if you were serving the Lord, not men, because you know that the Lord will reward everyone for whatever good he does, whether he is slave or free." The workplace needs compassion, and it needs servants.

Finding leaders who are willing to get their hands dirty, or to come out of their pristine offices to serve others is a rare occasion. If we are operating with integrity we should remember we are serving the Lord, not men. That can become a real challenge, especially as we have successes. The more we are told how great we are the harder it becomes to remember that God is great, not us.

To further understand the meaning of integrity, it is beneficial to identify what it means to *not* walk with integrity. It was just another hot muggy July day in Kansas City, or so I thought. Little did I know that this day I would remember for the rest of my life. Dennis and I were setting railroad ties in front of one of the townhouses we had helped build. With black sticky creosote on my hands, I took off my red ball cap to wipe the salty beads of perspiration from my forehead.

It was then that we heard the CB radio in the old red Ford truck nearby crackle.   "Dennis, would you have Rick come to the office? Greg would like to see him."

As I drew near the office I spotted Greg standing behind my old blue Chevy Malibu, writing down my license number. Immediately, my heart began pounding. *How could this be! Somehow he must have found out, I thought. Calm down, I told myself. Didn't Dennis say he'd been getting away with it for years?*

With a deep breath I reached for the knob of that flimsy, dirty white office door and pushed myself through to face Jerry and Greg. Greg, the owners' son, managed the business.

"Rick, did you buy gasoline for your car at the Mobil station and charge it to the company's account?" Greg asked without any pleasantries.

Oh no, I thought. *He did find out!* "No" I blurted.

"Rick, I've checked your license number to the Mobil receipts. According to their records you purchased gas there three times last month. We might not have caught it before, but we discontinued using our Mobil account last fall."

My face became hot, and I knew it was becoming red with embarrassment. How could I have been so stupid? My shoulders sagged as I recognized defeat. "You're right, Greg" I stated quietly.

"I hate to do this, Rick, because you've been a good employee, but I'm going to have to let you go, and you will have to repay these charges from your final paycheck."

I muttered, "I'm so sorry," as I turned to leave.

As I started my car I told myself that I never wanted to feel that embarrassment again. On occasions when tempted, since that day, I only have to remember the feelings I had standing there before Greg and Jerry, and the temptation becomes easier to overcome. Sometimes the best way to learn about integrity is to experience the humiliation of not walking *with* integrity.

Let's examine five common areas in which business people have a tendency to neglect their integrity. Later in this chapter we will identify steps to help correct these potential problem areas.

1. Taxes. Many business owners believe they have paid their fair share of taxes; therefore, it's okay for them to under-report their income, write-off expenses they never really spent, or take deductions they know are not deductible. Romans 13 highlights God's view on our responsibilities to the government. Meditate on this passage as you prepare your taxes. It might save your integrity.

Years ago I was waiting in the office of a car dealership that had sold me a brand new lemon. The owner, in front of several customers, announced to the bookkeeper that the IRS was coming on Monday, and it was time to pull out the phony set of books. This comment did not offer me great confidence in receiving satisfaction on my automotive complaint.

2. Billing practices. Overcharging customers, discriminatory pricing, or fraudulent billing will jeopardize a business's integrity. There are numerous ways that billing can be a problem. I recommend reviewing the method in your own business for any inconsistencies or deceit in your billing system.

A CPA firm I knew billed extra hours to their largest clients, when billable hours did not meet expectations. Even if the clients did not find out, the staff knew and always wondered when they might get drug into the mire.

3. Government regulations. Nothing slows entrepreneurs down or frustrates them more than government bureaucracy. When frustration levels rise people may have a tendency to circumvent regulations. Business leaders need to consider their integrity and their examples when they are tempted to break the rules.

As a junior accountant for a CPA firm I conducted government grant audits in small towns throughout Georgia. My job was to review payroll costs to ensure that the recipients of funds were not committing fraud. In one small town I discovered that the head of the local agency was paying his wife and daughter substantial salaries from government funds. The program specifically denied any form of nepotism (hiring family members).

I called the office I was reporting through and told the managing partner of my findings. After telling him the name of the fraud perpetrator I was shocked when he told me to pack up and come home. When I asked if we were going to do anything about this situation I was told that the suspect happened to be the brother of the government official who had hired the CPA firm.

My comment was, "So?"

"Come home, young man. We are not in the habit of biting the hand that feeds us," was the partner's reply.

As I continued to perform these audits the remainder of the summer it was hard for me to be excited about any discrepancies I found.

4. Kickbacks and bribes. Discerning the difference between a bribe or a kickback and a legitimate referral fee can be difficult. The American Heritage Dictionary of the English language defines bribe as, "Something, such as money or a favor, offered or given to a person in a position of trust to influence that person's views or conduct."

I attended a meeting once where an electrical contractor tried to convince his accountability group that payments he was making were not kickbacks. A salesman for a general contractor was steering work to this electrical contractor at a higher than normal margin in exchange for a payment to the salesman personally. The electrical contractor's entire staff knew about it and recognized it as a kickback. This had tarnished his testimony with his personnel, especially his bookkeeper. When the question was asked as to whether or not this electrical contractor would be willing to make that payment directly to the general contractor, rather than to the salesman, the light went on. The electrical contractor immediately repented and apologized to his staff. He has a much stronger testimony today.

5. *Software piracy*. It's very easy for a business to duplicate one purchased copy of software rather than pay for a site license or buy additional copies. This has become a growing multi-billion-dollar problem. It can be a very complicated issue.

Needing an upgraded version of Windows, I purchased a copy of Windows 95 from a retail store that normally sells closeouts and discounted products. After returning to my office I read the licensing agreement to find that a computer manufacturer had purchased this software originally. The limited license was only valid if the software was sold with the computer. I did not buy the computer, therefore it was not a legal license to me.

I returned the software for a refund to a puzzled and frustrated business owner. "I sell these all the time this way without a problem" was his comment. Fortunately, he was willing to refund my money.

Jesus taught, "If you love me, obey my commands." Love is the essence of integrity. If we love God we will walk with integrity. If we are truly living a life of integrity we will love others as well since Jesus told us to love others as we would ourselves. Integrity means living a life of loving God and others.

Benefits of Integrity

God invented the first bonus program. He knew that people only do what they get rewarded for doing. God desires obedience so He developed a bonus system to bless the faithful. Deuteronomy 28 describes this generous bonus plan.

In Deuteronomy God tells the Israelites that if they fully obey His commands He will bless them with the following benefits:

1. They would be set high above all nations of the earth.
2. They would be blessed in the city and in the country.
3. The fruit of their womb would be blessed.
4. The crops of their land and the young of their livestock would be blessed.
5. Their basket and kneading trough would be blessed.
6. They would be blessed when they come in and go out.
7. Their enemies would be defeated.
8. He would bless their barns and everything they put their hand to.
9. He would bless them in the land he would give them.
10. They would be established as His holy people.
11. They would be called by the name of the Lord and all peoples would fear them.
12. The Lord would grant them abundant prosperity.
13. He would open the heavens to send rain on their land in season.
14. He would bless all the work of their hands.
15. They would lend to many nations but borrow from none.
16. They would always be at the top not the bottom.

Wouldn't it be nice to experience those kinds of blessings? Can it happen? Not entirely. Notice this was a conditional promise— conditioned on *fully* obeying all of God's commands. No one but Jesus has measured up yet. God's nature has not changed. He still desires to reward his children's efforts, provided their efforts fall within God's will and give Him the glory.

Let's address some obvious questions that puzzle many people. Why do some righteous people fail? If a person is seeking to please God why is his business not prospering? Why do many wicked people prosper?

Job can help us determine some answers. Job was considered by God to be the most righteous man on earth at the time. Did he always prosper? No! He lost everything, except his grumbling wife. Did the world see him as a failure? Yes. Here's a man that had always been very prosperous and well respected. Suddenly not only did hard times come his way, but his friends kicked him while he was down and chastised him with their belief that his sin caused his problems.

Look at the end result for Job. He stuck with his integrity through it all. God reprimanded him for his complaining, but then in God's loving fashion, He restored prosperity to Job even greater than he previously experienced. The lesson here is that sometimes we have to be patient for prosperity, but in the meantime we should maintain our integrity.

Jesus loved to use farming as an example for His stories, because the people of that time could relate to working the land. The Bible teaches that we reap what we sow. Does that mean immediately? Not necessarily.

Let's examine closely the sowing and reaping process for growing crops. Farmers do not go to the field, plant their seeds, and return the same day for a harvest. Instead they have to work the ground to prepare it for the seed. They have to plant the seed and allow time for God to water the seed. Next, farmers remove the weeds and wait. As they monitor their crops, they gradually see the seeds sprouting and watch them grow. Eventually when the season is right they are able to harvest.

Business is very similar. There are seasons. When you first start you have to prepare like the farmer prepares the ground for the seeds. Next you have to plant lots of seeds. To generate income you have to do your sales and marketing activities, overcome objections, and convince prospects to buy. Eventually you move out of the seed planting phase and onto cultivating the bad things out of your business, refining your product and processes.

A company needs lots of sunshine and rain to make it grow. This equates to working hard for the customers. Sometimes it takes time for God to bless those efforts. Eventually if you've done the right things, and have worked hard, you begin to see some fruit from your efforts.

Many businesses fail before they reach the season of harvest. This can be due to poor planting, trying to work ground that is not tillable, or letting the weeds overrun the crop. Regardless of the reason we are not to try the shortcuts of giving up our integrity. This will just cause eternal ruin.

As far as the wicked that prosper, they also reap what they sow. If their entire motivation is to make money, they may become very good at planting those types of seed, weeding out the problems, and working the land. They will not, however, reap any eternal harvest.

God is so compassionate He may allow the wicked their desires here on earth, knowing that they will not experience pleasure after death. Remember Jesus' parable of Lazarus and the rich man? In Luke 16:25 Jesus said, "Son, remember that in your lifetime you received your good things, while Lazarus received bad things, but now he is comforted here and you are in agony."

There are other benefits of integrity not listed in Deuteronomy. Peace of mind is one. If you walk with integrity, then you will not have trouble sleeping at night. Your conscience will be clear. You will not have to continually wonder what lie you last told to whom. It's amazing how a lie begets a lie until finally it all comes crumbling down. God desires to give us that peace that passes all understanding. With righteousness as a guide we can attain that kind of peace.

Integrity earns the respect of others. Have you ever met someone with whom you have no reservations— someone you would trust with anything you own? Examine that person's traits and model them. God wants you to conduct yourself in this fashion. Integrity fosters trust that will prosper your business.

Imagine what you would do if pipes suddenly burst in your house. As the water gushes down the hallways you search the yellow pages for a plumber. Two plumbers are near you—one who has an excellent reputation, but charges more, while the other one took advantage of you last time and sold you parts that you later found were unnecessary. Which one are you going to call?

Over time this, too, can happen in your business. People will pay more and come back to you if you have proven they can trust you. If we truly want to please God we need to walk before Him with integrity. If we sow righteousness we will eventually reap blessings.

How to Implement

Hopefully you now see that the benefits of walking with integrity far outweigh the costs. Are *you* walking with integrity? Personally, I always strive to do better. How do you go about implementing integrity into your life? I have developed a few steps that should help.

Step 1: *Review Your Current Practices-* Identify any weaknesses. Examine yourself first, and then survey your employees and customers to determine any shortcomings or inappropriateness.

The first area to review is your personal relationship with God. Are you growing in your knowledge and understanding of God's nature? We are typically a people of action, taking very little time with God. If you want to lead with integrity you need to know the nature of God, and to be willing to spend enough time with the Creator to know His design for your business.

Remember the contractor I mentioned earlier who didn't even recognize his kickback as wrong? Sometimes we need an outside objective opinion to identify all of our weaknesses. Take your review beyond yourself. Seek other people's input on your potential weaknesses.

Step 2: *Develop Your Desired Values-* Think about your business and what values are important to God, to you, and to your business. Review the Ten Commandments, Leviticus 19, and Proverbs to determine which values should be instilled in all your employees.

Step 3: *Communicate Your Desired Values-* Communicate your desired values emphatically and often. Many studies reveal a correlation between companies with known solid values and their enhanced profitability. Be creative. Use plaques, notes with pay stubs, or whatever ways you determine will best consistently convey these values.

Step 4: *Make a Commitment to These Values-* Commit to God and yourself to uphold these values in your own life and business. Find people to hold you accountable to your commitment and develop ways to hold your staff accountable to them as well.

The Old Testament speaks many times of markers that the Israelites would place in strategic locations to reflect the commitment they had made to God. A covenant or marker in your business may be what it takes to remember your commitments. In my office I have a Bible verse (I Kings 9:4-5) on the wall that reminds me of a commitment I have made to the Lord about obeying His commands. It's a great reminder to review periodically.

Step 5: *Model the values-* If you do not demonstrate these values each and every day, even in small things, your employees will not take you seriously. Soon they will be following your poor example, not what you wish them to do. When you fall it is just as important to admit your mistakes, learn from them, then keep moving forward. No one will get it right each time, but if we humbly admit our mistakes our leadership will be solidified and respected.

If you examine your business's integrity, follow the above steps, and focus on relationships first, you will be on your way to fulfilling God's mission for your company. These things will bear more fruit eternally than all of the profits you could produce.

If you have children you know how quickly they mimic their parents behavior. If they see us throwing temper tantrums it's hard to reprimand them when they do. The workplace is not any different.

How to Monitor

Integrity is not a one-time deal. Every day you have to start fresh, striving to walk the path of righteousness. You can be full of integrity and be deceived by Satan or your flesh.

An associate pastor known to me became enamored with a young lady attending the school housed in his church. He began writing her inappropriate notes. This pastor had what appeared to be a very strong marriage and was a very kind shepherd and teacher. His flesh unfortunately got the better of him. This tragic event drove this man out of the ministry, and put a tremendous strain on his family and his self-worth.

Since even the best of us has a sinful nature it is absolutely essential that we determine a way to monitor our integrity. Let me make some suggestions:

1. Regular quiet time with the Lord. If we remain constantly in the presence of God it is more difficult for us to ignore the areas that God may be working on in our lives.

2. Schedule periodic, but regular retreats with God. Even our daily quiet time is not enough. It's too easy to race through a brief devotional or say a quick prayer and then get on with our day. If you try to schedule a regular time to go away in solitude for at least half a day with the Lord you will attend to those areas of your life that need addressing.

3. Be accountable. Find some friends who love you enough to hold you accountable. Meet with them regularly and ask one another tough questions. Rod Handley of Character That Counts has written an excellent book on this subject called *Character Counts, Who's Counting Yours?* It gives practical steps in starting an accountability group and what questions to ask.

4. Tell people about your desire to live with integrity. If people around you such as your staff, family, suppliers, or customers know you truly desire to do what is right, they will be more likely to hold you accountable.

Earlier I shared the story about the electrical contractor and a kickback. This issue may never have surfaced. He wanted to walk with integrity enough that he asked his top manager to speak to his accountability group privately and answer any of their questions honestly. It was through this dialogue that the kickback issue surfaced. At the risk of losing his job this manager cared enough about his boss to disclose this sensitive issue.

When my former partner and I started Integrity

Management, a biblically based management consulting practice that evolved into a ministry called Integrity Resource Center, one of the hardest things we had to do was name the business. We agonized over that decision for weeks. We examined many names and sought counsel. Finally we narrowed it down to two names. One of them had the word Christian in it, and the other was Integrity Management.

The Lord finally gave us a sense of peace that it should be called Integrity Management. Several months later during my quiet time I thought about the process of naming our business. In the quiet of the morning the Lord gave me this keen insight. "Rick, I could have let you name the business Christian, and maybe Christians would have held you accountable, but I had you name it Integrity because I wanted the whole world to hold you accountable." I don't always measure up but the name has helped keep me on track. Try accountability. You will find it easier to stay on the right path.

Walking with integrity is not easy or popular. If you develop and maintain a close intimate relationship with our Lord and Savior, and stop and reflect on the consequences of your actions, both now and eternally, before leaving the path of righteousness, your journey should be a more prosperous one.

Beyond Excellence

"Whatever you do, work at it with all your heart, as working for the Lord, not for men, since you know that you will receive an inheritance from the Lord as a reward. It is the Lord Christ you are serving." Colossians 3:23-24

The world's purpose in achieving excellence in business is typically profit motivated, while the biblical purpose of excellence is to *glorify God.* Jesus taught "Be perfect, as your heavenly Father is perfect."

Scripture calls us to labor as if our work is for God not men, *because it is for God.* If Jesus were coming to your house would you leave the china in the cabinet? Would you serve him hot dogs instead of steak? If Jesus came to your business would you sell him your seconds, or provide him with inferior service? I would hope not.

Your work matters, whether you are serving Jesus, or your least profitable customer. Ephesians 2:10 teaches, "For we are God's workmanship, created in Christ Jesus to do good works, which God prepared in advance for us to do."

Consider the impact of that verse. The work you are involved in was prepared by God for you to do, and to do it well! Recognizing your work as a calling from God, and as an act of worship, will give you a whole new perspective on excellence.

If your concept of excellence flows from your desire for increased profitability, you will eventually cut corners. If you are serving a customer who doesn't demand, or expect, as much as others, you may be tempted to give them second best. If instead your motive for excellence flows from recognizing that the act itself is an appointed act of worship to God, you will be more likely to consistently apply excellence in your business.

What is Excellence?

Over the years I have worked with many lawn and land-scaping businesses. Most of them, especially in their initial stages, use old, run-down trucks, buy used equipment, and store it in an old shed by their house. When you examine their service it is often done adequately, but without much attention to the details that make a business stand out.

Larry is different. He began his lawn and landscaping business the same year we moved into our house. We were one of his first customers. From the very beginning it was easy to see that Larry's business was different.

He had a nice red truck with his company name neatly printed on the side. His equipment was always well main-tained, and his service typically exceeded expectations. He particularly was good at communicating. He would perform his service, and leave a note on the door with specific instruc-tions and helpful information to assist our lawn to become the best we were willing it to be.

After 15 years of watching Larry's business flourish, I had the opportunity to tour his business. His attentiveness to detail was evident everywhere. His staff, his facility, and his processes and procedures were excellent.

To maintain a large facility spotlessly is no easy accom-plishment in a business involved with lots of fertilizer, seed, and tools, but Larry has developed habits personally to model his expectation for excellence. Over lunch I noted that wher-ever we were Larry went out of his way to pick up trash in other people's property, and to attend to details that would not matter to most people.

Larry knows that God equipped and designed him for this very act of worship. He has modeled excellence to the staff, and they have risen to the challenge in complying. A nice byproduct of his pursuit of excellence is the ability to charge premium prices for his service, and his customers gladly pay it, because they know he will be reliable.

The D.K. Illustrated Oxford Dictionary defines excel as being superior or preeminent. Some people mistake excel-lence for the need to have the very best. We don't need to drive a Rolls Royce to achieve excellence, but what we do drive should be well maintained. When I think of Jesus I think of someone who did not have a home, or the latest style of clothes, but I suspect that everything he owned was well maintained.

Excellence in your business should tell the world that you are serving God with class: first class service, first class quality, and first class products. Not necessarily the most expensive, just first class.

If you reflect excellence in your business you will be proud of your service, products, facilities, staff, and your reputation. Slothfulness in business can make excellence unachievable. Excellence requires commitment, both in money and in time. This commitment however pays dividends.

Your reputation will speak for itself, your employees will be pleased to sell your products or services, and your customers will be many. But most of all God will be pleased with your living sacrifice, offered up as holy and pleasing to God—a spiritual act of worship. (Romans 12:1,2)

How Do You Establish Excellence in Your Business

It's not easy achieving excellence in business, but neither is following Christ. In almost any business there are phone calls, paperwork, employee issues, order processing, and more. If any of these items are handled poorly your reputation suffers. *Excellence comes from handling the details well, and with passion.*

If you desire your business to be a model of excellence first determine what excellence should look like. Don't stop with just the customers' perspective. Examine all facets of your business. Whether it is your sales and marketing, accounting and finance, operations, or management areas, you should identify the attributes necessary to achieve excellence in each department.

Take time to pause and reflect on each of these key business areas. Picture it in your mind, and then write down your overall vision of excellence for the business. How would your customers define excellence? What about your staff? Vendors?

Explore each department, and each process, with your staff. Solicit their feedback on what steps they can take in their respective areas that would improve their departments, striving towards the overall goal of excellence.

Ask yourself and your staff, if Jesus came into their department, or bought your product or service, would He be impressed or disappointed? From these discussions and thoughts, develop a collective idea of excellence for each process and department. Make the picture as tangible as possible.

Once you have a clear vision of excellence you need to cast that vision for your employees. Give them a passion for excellence. Assure them of your commitment to the new standards for your business. Look for opportunities to lead by example. If you show a willingness to invest money in providing excellence your staff will follow.

Once the vision is cast set goals for yourself and your staff. Establish goals that are specific and measurable. Track the actual results and compare them to the goals on a regular basis. Hold people accountable to those goals, and consider rewards and penalties when goals are exceeded, or not met respectively.

To be successful at implementing excellence in your business it is necessary that you take the lead, and not waver when excellence costs you money; support your staff's attempts at achieving the goals you've established; and most of all remember excellence comes as much from attitude as it does hard work.

As usual the Bible has some excellent guidelines for this process. Paul gave some direction to slaves and masters in Ephesians 6:5-9, "Slaves, obey your earthly masters with *respect* and *fear*, and with *sincerity of heart*, just as you would obey Christ. Obey them not only to win their favor when their eye is on you, but like slaves of Christ, doing the will of God from your heart. *Serve wholeheartedly*, as if you were serving the Lord, not men, because you know that the Lord will reward everyone for whatever good he does, whether he is slave or free. And masters, treat your slaves in the same way. (emphasis added.)"

In this passage the items helpful in establishing excellence include "sincerity of heart" and "respect and fear" of authority. It is difficult to attend to details unless you do it with sincerity of heart. Hiring well is critical! Everyone has certain passions in life. If the people you hire are not particularly passionate about their career, then the excellence of the business as a whole will suffer.

This passion also needs to be modeled by leadership, and emphasized to the staff. If the staff does not understand the importance of their job in respect to the big picture it will be difficult for them to be passionate about their results. If you recognize and acknowledge the value of each person's job, they soon will as well.

If respect and fear of the proper authorities, including management and God, are modeled and set as the standard, excellence will come easier. This, combined with serving wholeheartedly, will lead to God being pleased with our work.

How To Maintain Excellence

Since our workplaces are full of flawed individuals we will never reach perfection. To maintain corporate wide excellence it will require procedures, policies, constant monitoring, and a great measure of grace. It's easier at times to be slothful and let quality slide.

A growing business requires us to rely on others. When they do not perform up to our expectations it can become frustrating. Tolerating a lower standard becomes an attractive option. Please don't fall into this trap.

Satan would like nothing more than to have you fall into his snare of complacency and helplessness. If you are a business leader then God has given you the authority, and He will also give you the ability to excel.

One caution needs to be emphasized for you overachievers. Excellence does not mean perfection. Striving for perfection can lead to overload. Excellence needs to be balanced with God's direction in Psalm 127:1-2, "Unless the Lord builds the house, its builders labor in vain. Unless the Lord watches over the city, the watchmen stand guard in vain. In vain you rise early and stay up late, toiling for food to eat—for he grants sleep to those he loves."

If you are an overachiever you might consider putting limits on yourself, and on your employees, as to total number of hours worked each week. You will also need to assure that you are working on God's house, rather than your own. Prayerfully consider your priorities, and make sure your activities line up with God's plan.

To achieve excellence you have to start with yourself. Are you maintaining the level of excellence that you know God desires? A periodic review of your progress will be necessary. You will also need some form of accountability. Write down your standards of excellence that you desire to maintain. Give a copy to someone close to you that loves you enough to hold you accountable.

Another bold move would be to give it to your key employees and ask them to hold you accountable. This will help them see the commitment that you have to these standards, which will likely improve their performance as they try and mirror your desires.

After you have set yourself up with standards of excellence, and some form of accountability, then you can begin with your staff. The criterion of excellence that you have in mind should be clearly conveyed to each staff member. The staff should also know exactly how their individual job is affected by these guidelines. Incorporate these standards into their job description, and hold them accountable by measuring their effectiveness. Reward them accordingly.

Another effective way in maintaining the desired standards of excellence is to survey your customers. Feedback from patrons is necessary to determine if you are exceeding their expectations. Ask them what they like, and what they don't like, about your products or services.

Take the results seriously, and have a follow up plan as to how you implement the suggestions you receive from these surveys. You might also want to consider surveying suppliers and employees as well.

Maintaining excellence will usually require that you actually raise the bar periodically. What seems excellent today usually becomes obsolete tomorrow if you don't look for ways to raise the standard, and provide new and improved products or services.

Consider the mail system as an example. If everyone had continued surviving with the postal system as it was, without dreaming of something better the fax machine may never have been invented, or Federal Express would have never been born. Constant forward thinking about the next level in your business will keep you ahead of the paradigm shifts that have left so many businesses behind, and ultimately led them to destruction.

How To Measure Excellence

Excellence can be somewhat esoteric. You may know it when you see it, but measuring the degree of quality can be a challenge. Each person may have different standards, but there are usually common benchmarks to be applied.

It can be helpful to survey customers, employees, and suppliers. A quantitative survey can give you tangible results that will let you know how your business measures up to the expectations of these groups of people. Taking these results seriously and implementing changes where necessary will certainly help improve your standard of excellence.

As an owner or manager it is good to test your products and services when possible. This will give you first hand knowledge. Many times customers are treated poorly via the phone.

This is something that you can test yourself to see if the staff is friendly, courteous, and helpful. Informally, you can also ask friends to test your company to get their feedback. Some businesses, especially banks, even use mystery shoppers. These people, unknowingly to the staff, come in and establish a customer relationship and then let management know the detailed results.

Another way to gauge your level of excellence is by tracking the number of complaints, and positive responses, you receive from customers. We can't always be perfect, so we naturally are going to have people that complain from time to time. These complaints can actually be your best opportunity to fix problems in your operation, and if handled properly can also be a great chance to turn that customer from an angry and unhappy one to a loyal, impressed customer.

You should learn to cherish the customers that complain. For every one of them that has the courage to complain, you probably have four or five quietly walking out the door swearing that they will never come back.

Focus groups are another way to determine customer response before investing the money to roll out a new product or service. These can be very valuable. I worked for a bank that had a tendency towards developing products based on their operational abilities and capacities, without much concern for what the customer desired. This bank was ready to roll out a new product, which once again was primarily going to be operationally driven, when someone had the idea to try it out on a focus group.

The focus group discarded their idea, and actually suggested a packaged product that would include several key features rolled into one account. Management actually listened this time, and developed the product exactly the way the customers desired. It was tremendously successful.

To go beyond excellence requires setting very high standards, God sized standards, effectively implementing the standards, measuring your success, and maintaining a level of satisfaction and balance far above your industry. This will take prayer, hard work, diligence, patience, and a clear vision, but the result will be pleasing to God.

A Mission Higher than Profits

"So do not worry, saying, 'What shall we eat?' or 'What shall we drink?' or
'What shall we wear?' For the pagans run after all these things, and your
heavenly Father knows that you need them. But seek first his kingdom and
his righteousness, and all these things will be given to you as well."
Matthew 6:31-33

It does not make sense that if you invest time and money
in non income producing activities like evangelism and discipleship that you will still have your needs met, but that is
exactly what Jesus was saying in Matthew 6:31-33. Few
Christians in business recognize the higher calling God has
for them in and through their business. This is partially
because it doesn't make sense to them. Mixing the spiritual
with business seems to be a dangerous move to many, without any possibility of payback.

What confounds men, however, is perfectly reasonable to
God. I was reminded of Jesus' principle recently, "you reap
what you sow." After praying for inexpensive help to change
our website, I was pleasantly surprised when an acquaintance
stopped me after a meeting.

He informed me that he felt God instructed him to help
my ministry. As he explained further it turned out that he
wanted to give of his business time to some ministries, and
ours had been one he felt led to choose. He refused to take
payment for developing our website, some marketing materials, and some good advice. In my mind he sowed some pretty
good seeds for our ministry, so I was obliged to refer business
to him when I could. Over the next couple of months God
gave me the opportunity to refer some good accounts to his
company, a harvest he hadn't counted on.

If you desire to lead a business with integrity you need to
sow eternal seed generously. Business is not just about profits.
Yes, you need to be profitable for the long-term success of

your business, but God calls us to a higher standard. He has a mission higher than profits for each business.

Developing a Ministry Plan

Business leaders typically recognize the value in having a business plan. They will work through a strategic plan occasionally, they may also have a marketing plan developed, but very few have ever considered developing a *ministry* plan for their business.

Like any plan, a ministry plan can help you become purposeful about developing goals and action plans for the future of your business. The kinds of goals, however, are uniquely different. A ministry plan will focus you on how you can have eternal significance in and through your business, rather than the temporal, profit-motivated plans that are so commonplace in the business community.

This concept of a ministry plan may make you uncomfortable. It certainly is not for the faint hearted. A ministry plan requires leaving our comfort zone, and it comes with risks. The rewards however are eternal and significant. Incredible things can and do happen when God's people open their workplace to His work.

A ministry plan should begin with an *objective*. What is it overall you hope to accomplish? It doesn't have to be anything fancy. Just succinctly and plainly stating your desired outcome of performing ministry through your business will allow you as a business to remain focused on the important eternal tasks for which you have been called.

After your objective has been stated you need to dig into the meat of the plan. Your plan should concentrate on five key areas addressed in scripture: Evangelism, Discipleship, Ministering to your Employees, Ministering to the oppressed, and Ministering to others. In each section of your plan, outline your purpose for focusing on this activity, and the acceptable and unacceptable methods to accomplish your goals.

Evangelism

In Matthew 28:19 Jesus told His disciples, "Therefore go and make disciples of all nations, baptizing them in the name of the Father and of the Son and of the Holy Spirit." This was one of Jesus' last instructions. It was the essence of his mission to not only be the sacrifice that would atone for our sins, but also to begin the process of spreading the Good News of the Gospel. This is a charge for each and every believer in Jesus that is applicable today as much as it was back then.

The workplace is ripe for the harvest, but as in Jesus' time the workers are few. As business leaders we have a tremendous opportunity to share the gospel with many people who never enter a place of worship. Unfortunately, this platform is seriously underutilized. Too many Christians are quick to appoint their pastor as the one who should save souls.

Jesus could have appointed and anointed the clergy of the day to build the church and to preach the gospel, instead he told a bunch of fishermen, a tax collector, and other assorted people of commerce to go forth and preach the gospel. We need to recognize our call, and be obedient to that call, and quit hiding behind our rationalizations for avoiding this difficult but very exciting possibility.

Why is this so difficult? I believe there are several reasons for our shortcomings as evangelists. One primary reason is fear. We often times are afraid of what others will think.

Pastor D. James Kennedy on one of his radio broadcasts painted a word picture of someone watching their neighbor's house go up in flames, knowing the whole time that their neighbor is asleep inside. Would you go wake them, or would you be afraid to make them mad that you woke them up? The point is that naturally you wouldn't let them burn to death, if it was within your ability to save them. Yet we avoid almost each day the opportunity to save people from a far worse and everlasting fate, by refusing to share the gospel with the lost.

Another reason for falling short in evangelism is a lack of knowledge. Many of us are not comfortable that we will know the right verses to discuss, or have all the answers to their questions. This assumes that we are on our own, rather than being led by the Holy Spirit.

If lack of knowledge is a legitimate concern then you should be willing to get trained. If you wanted to become a lawyer you wouldn't go apply for a job without a law degree. Likewise, if you realize that Jesus called all believers to evangelize, then it is your duty to get appropriate training to be equipped to help someone avoid the lake of fire.

When God is leading, you never have to worry about the method you use to save the lost, but it is beneficial to be prepared to give a reason for the faith that is within you. To assist you, I asked Mark Lockard, owner of Crescent Cleaners in Harrisonville, Missouri, to share some pointers he has learned over the years to effectively present the gospel to his employees and in the marketplace.

Mark has a gift and a heart for evangelism, and has been used by God in a powerful way in the lives of many people. The following points are foundational items necessary to effectively presenting the gospel.

1. Know your own story. Be prepared to tell your story of salvation quickly and effectively. Mark recommends that you divide your life-story into three parts: Before Christ, Conversion experience, and After Christ. This will help you to be prepared to share your personal experience effectively.

2. Pray for opportunities. Pray that God would give you soul-winning eyes that do not overlook opportunities. Pray also for a sensitive heart, willing to respond to needs and opportunities. Pray for courage, and for a ripe harvest.

3. Stay in a close intimate relationship with Him. Experience God's glory yourself. People can't catch what you don't have.

4. Respond out of relationship. God draws people to Himself. Our job is to recognize whom God is drawing, and be ready and willing to respond.

5. Develop relationships by sharing God's love. Look for opportunities to share God's love to a lost and hurting world. Listen to others, and take time to go out of your way for others.

6. Have a plan. Know the method or tools you are going

to use when God presents you with an opportunity. Be sensitive and flexible in your method, and make sure the method doesn't get in the way. Relate the gospel to their specific need.

7. **Be purposeful and intentional.** Make appointments, and invite others to lunch or dinner, church, etc. Look for ways to spend time with them to earn the right to share Christ. Pray that God would enable you to live an upright life.

Mark also has a few valuable thoughts on steps to take, and methods he has used that may prove helpful.

1. **Listen, relate, and care for others.** Be sensitive to their background, experiences, and current issues.

2. **Ask for permission to share after listening.** This approach is less threatening and diffuses tension.

3. **Establish the authority of the Bible.** People are looking for some authority they can trust. Ask if you can share scripture so they know that the truths aren't coming from you.

4. **Consider using the Romans Road to Salvation.** Romans 3:10, 23 points out they are sinners. Romans 5:8 and 6:23 gives them the good news that Jesus died for us. Romans 10:9-10, 13 points them towards confession and the plan of salvation. Close with Revelation 3:20. God is knocking at their door, what is their decision.

5. **Interject personal illustrations of what God has done for you.** This makes your story more relevant.

6. **Be humble and let them know you have faults as well.** God loves us in spite of our flaws.

7. **Ask if they would like to pray to assure their salvation.** They may need to process information before they are willing. Be gentle and leave the door open for further discussions.

8. **If possible give them something tangible, to remind them physically of their commitment.** Writing on the back of a tract or card a recap of their commitment with your signature as a witness may give them something to cling to when times get hard.

9. **Move them from an experience to an ongoing relationship.** They need to be discipled immediately. If possible start them on an introductory bible study. The Nazarene

church has an eight-week study that's good for this purpose. Christian Business Men's Committee (CBMC) also has a series called Operation Timothy that is good for this stage. Plug them into a healthy church as soon as possible.

10. Consider personalizing their experience by buying them a Bible with their name embossed on it. My friend Mark orders them a Life Application Bible with index tabs and their name on it. He tells them it has been personalized, because that's the kind of relationship God wants to have with them. He also lists the scriptures for the Romans Road to Salvation on the title page of Romans, and underlines these scriptures in green to emphasize new life. He challenges them to use this in the future to evangelize to others.

Evangelism can be tough enough without confusing the matter further with workplace issues. The balance of trying to run a profitable business, while balancing it with the opportunities that come up to share the gospel with others, can be trying. To complicate it further can be the issue of employer/employee relations. Many employees will feel that you expect them to submit to your ideas as their employer. Salvation doesn't come through coercion. God designed it to be a willing choice. Be sensitive to their concerns.

You also need to be sensitive to legal issues that come with workplace evangelism. The American Center for Law and Justice in their booklet titled "Christian Rights in the Workplace" states that, "An employer can talk about his religious beliefs with employees as long as employees know that continued employment or advancement within the company is not conditioned upon acquiescence in the employer's religious beliefs....Employers must be careful, however, not to persist in witnessing if the employee objects. Such unwanted proselytizing could be deemed religious harassment."

Discipleship

A good shepherd assures that his flock has its needs met, this applies spiritually as well as physically. A portion of your ministry plan should address your employees' need for spiritual growth. If you have brand new believers they naturally need to be discipled and steered towards a strong relationship with the Lord. Existing believers also need to be continually challenged in growing in their relationship with the Lord, and applying God's truth to their daily environment.

Discipleship can take place on a one on one basis or in a group setting. Many businesses have voluntary Bible study groups meeting in their office before or after work hours, or during break times. This can be an easy way to encourage employees to go deeper into the Word, and hear more from you about the beliefs that you value, and how they practically can be applied in the workplace. Just be sure that employees recognize that the activity is voluntary, and is being held outside of work hours.

In your ministry plan address the methodologies you are willing to use, and what is not acceptable, so that your boundaries are well defined. Encourage other believers in your workplace to disciple others as well. The real fruit comes when you are able to have more than one person in the workplace actively practicing and teaching God's Word to others as well.

Ministering to Your Employees

Hand in hand with evangelism and discipleship is ministering to the needs of your employees. 1 Timothy 5:8 teaches, "If anyone does not provide for his relatives, and especially for his immediate family, he has denied the faith and is worse than an unbeliever." The principle behind this passage is that we are to take care of our own. For a business leader this means God has placed people in your care for a reason, and they should be treated as your "business family."

People have many needs that range from the emotional, physical, psychological, and the spiritual. If you ignore these needs you not only will damage your opportunity to evangelize and disciple these people, but you will also be shirking your responsibility as the steward over these people. Jesus' most effective ministry came from his willingness to meet the individual needs of the people, both physically and spiritually.

There are many different ways to minister to your

employees, but the most important way is to be available and sensitive to listening when they have issues they feel need addressed. Setting up an employee assistance fund has been one method I have seen used effectively. These funds can be designed to help the needy among you. Maybe someone is about to have their utilities shut off, or have a house foreclosed on, or medical bills have sent them reeling. These are all opportunities to show the love of Christ by having either the company, or other employees, or preferably both pitching in to help them in their time of need.

Marketplace Ministries has a chaplain program that many companies use to provide an outlet for their employees. These chaplains are able to help employees with family tragedies, weddings, funerals, addictions, and many other issues, which may be important to them. This can be a non-threatening way for an employer to provide spiritual counsel at a time when the employee is willing to hear, without the employee feeling job pressure, because of it coming from their boss.

Be creative in finding ways to meet the ongoing needs of your staff. They will appreciate it, and it will likely bear eternal rewards.

Ministering to the Oppressed

Employees have needs, but so do the people of your community. In Leviticus 19:9-10 God commanded the Israelites, "When you reap the harvest of your land, do not reap to the very edges of your field or gather the gleanings of your harvest. Do not go over your vineyard a second time or pick up the grapes that have fallen. Leave them for the poor and the alien. I am the Lord your God."

God desires us to use our businesses to give from our excess to help the poor, aliens (unbelievers), and widows and orphans. (See James 1:27) We need to be obedient to this standard by using our business resources to assist with the needs of the community. Businesses have the unique opportunity to use their people and their time to be very effective. Unfortunately, we see large Fortune 500 businesses leveraging this strength for activities that do not always glorify God, while many smaller businesses that have a heart for God's work overlook this creative way to assist the community and do it for God's glory.

Look for activities that your business could assist in that would meet the needs of these oppressed classes of people. One area of blight in our culture today is the single parent. They are similar to the widows of the biblical times. They have limited resources and big responsibilities without near enough help. God would be pleased to see us use our time, talent, and money to help these hurting people in our community.

Ministering to Others

Businesses have tremendous influence in their community. They make daily contact with customers, suppliers, civic organizations, politicians, and many public servants. These are all opportunities to make disciples for Jesus Christ. Demonstrating excellence in all that you do, loving others, and serving others can change the very nature of your city.

A pastor recently shared a story with me about a group of business owners who came together to talk about using their business to God's glory. The pastor challenged them to begin praying for their competition. Rather than view them as an enemy, he challenged these men to love them. The next week one of these men did.

It seems he had been so convicted by that conversation that he went home and called his competitor. He apologized to this man for the times he had degraded him to prospective customers. He went a step further and said that his company would no longer say derogatory things about their competition, and would actually begin referring customers to them when they were a more suitable solution. The very next day both parties referred customers to each other, and began working towards making their industry and businesses more cooperative and stronger.

God would like you to consider in your ministry plan how you can better serve others. Whether it is your competition, your customers, your suppliers, or just other business people, look for ways to shine the light of Christ into their lives. Solicit input from your staff as to how you can better accomplish this noble goal.

Summary

A ministry plan can be a scary thought. It takes a large leap of faith. It also requires that your faith become real not only to you, but also to the staff around you. If you properly outline your goals and objectives, communicate them to your staff, and then model them I think you will be amazed at how God will honor your efforts. The harvest is ripe, but the workers are few. Are you up for the challenge?

Accountability

"Two are better than one, because they have a good return for their work:
If one falls down his friend can help him up. But pity the man who falls
and has no one to help him up!" Ecclesiastes 4:9,10

It was in a motel room in San Antonio, Texas when I realized that God was calling me to become an entrepreneur once again. After my car rental agency I had promised myself that I would never again try to be an entrepreneur. I have many shortcomings and I knew that starting something from scratch was one of them.

Thinking more about *my* abilities, or I should say my lack of abilities, rather than God's ability, I spent the weekend struggling with God over his desire for me to begin a ministry to business owners. Looking back I think I had a taste of what Moses felt when God told him to go to Pharaoh. I spent the weekend trying to convince God that he had the wrong man. By the end of the weekend God won out. I left that motel knowing that God had assured me that he would provide for the areas in which I felt weak if I would just commit to his plan. I agreed.

When I returned home the first phone call I received was from Gregg. Gregg told me that he and his wife had stayed up much of the night praying about his career. He felt that God wanted him to leave the bank and to help me begin a financial ministry to businesses. Gregg has a lot of skills in which I feel I lack. What I didn't know until a couple of years later is that my wife had spoken with Gregg over that weekend and she had told him that she felt that he and I should go together to start a ministry.

Gregg gave me the courage to press ahead. He laid much of the foundation of Integrity Management on solid biblical principles. He also was there to support my wife, Kathy, and me while Kathy had to suffer through chemotherapy for breast cancer. Gregg was the accountability partner that I needed to actually move forward with Integrity Management.

Accountability is a word that you won't find in the Bible often, if at all. The *principle* of accountability, however, you will find in many passages. Solomon in Ecclesiastes told us "Iron sharpens Iron as one man sharpens another." Romans 13 clearly describes God's lines of authority and His expectation that we submit to the authorities that He has placed over us. God gives us sound principles, not to punish us, but because He knows our sinful nature, and He knows what we need to stay on course.

Imagine living in a place that had absolutely no accountability: no police, no judges, no pastors, no bosses, and no spouses. What an incredible picture of chaos that would be. If you dwell on that possibility you will see quickly why in this fallen world we need accountability in all facets of our life.

Business is no different. Many people start businesses because of their desire to run away from their current accountability structure. In our culture today we encourage this activity. We love the independence of being our own boss, or starting our own church without being shackled by a denomination. Is this God's plan? Many times I think not.

The new business owner is often times very frustrated to find that they may have run away from their current accountability structure right into the arms of a bigger and more complex accountability structure. The IRS, the city government, the state unemployment department, the federal unemployment department, the state government, a board of directors, your employees all hold you accountable to regulations, rules and responsibilities of which you never dreamed. Although this excessive regulation seems bad, and sometimes it may be, God wants us accountable to others because he knows our shortcomings.

Why do we need accountability?

If you want long-term prosperity, God's way, you need help. Our flesh is too weak to stand alone. There are many other reasons, as well, why God wants us accountable to someone. Here are a few.

- Our sinful nature needs to be examined objectively.
- We need another source of wisdom when God isn't getting our attention.
- To put order in a chaotic world.
- We need to learn humility.
- We gain different perspectives.
- It is a way to distribute wealth to others in need.
- Protection.

A business owner told me about his plans to begin buying businesses in related fields, so that he could integrate his products and services with the expanded client base. He intended to go on an acquisition binge even though he had questionable capital resources to fulfill his dream.

The next time I saw him I asked how his acquisition plans were coming along. He shared this story. While unveiling his plans to his board a wise board member asked him, are you doing this for your ego or for the good of the company? This wise counselor explained that in his opinion it would make much more sense to form strategic alliances with these companies rather than buy them.

The business owner told me that at first it bruised his ego to be questioned about his motives and it made him angry, but after he went home and prayed and reflected on it that evening he realized that his original motives were not pure. He took this wise man's advice and is confident that this counsel saved his business potentially millions of dollars that may have been lost in the pursuit of his dream.

God needs others to work through when we are not listening to him, or when our desires have replaced God's rightful place on the throne. Accountability in a business is imperative for the success of the business, as well as for the success of those with whom it comes in contact. Without accountability it becomes a place of chaos.

To whom should we be accountable?

In business there are people or institutions to which we have no choice but to be accountable, the government for instance. There are also people or institutions to which we should be accountable, but we do have a choice. The church is an example. As a business owner we are accountable to our board, if we have one. We are accountable to our spouse and family in providing for their needs, we are accountable to the government for taxes and complying with regulations, and we should be accountable to the church.

We always have a choice, but if we make a bad choice we may find ourselves in jail. I have worked with many businesses that have decided not to pay the IRS payroll taxes when due. Eventually, the IRS either gets their attention with penalties and interest, or if necessary, by closing their business. We do have a choice to whom we *desire* to be accountable, and to whom we don't necessarily *have* to be accountable. But just like the IRS, you can pay now or pay later. If you choose to be a maverick, without any personal accountability, you will eventually cause yourself to stumble and it will cost you dearly.

Spouse

Very few business owners even consider being accountable to their spouse in their business. You might wonder why should you be accountable to your spouse? After all, many of our spouses don't understand our business. Regardless of the degree of knowledge your spouse may have you owe it to your spouse to include them in your major business decisions. It usually is unwise to proceed without their agreement. Let me explain.

The Lord knew long before you did whom your perfect mate should be. He knew your strengths and your weaknesses; he knew how you think, and the things that you overlook. Since in His infinite wisdom He knew these things He wanted to provide you with a helpmate that could offset your deficiencies.

If you examine closely your spouse's strengths and weaknesses they are typically strong where you are weak and weak where you are strong. If you're a visionary, they may be a detail person. If you have poor judgment they are likely to have good judgment. If you do not consult with this gift from God, it is very likely that you will make decisions without considering all of the necessary factors. Different perspectives are necessary to analyze tough situations, and it calls for having as much wisdom as possible. Don't pass up some of the best wisdom you will ever find.

My wife is not a businessperson. When we were first married I would turn on the nightly business report around bedtime. Kathy would try to stay up with me, but out of boredom within minutes she would be sound asleep. Although she does not understand the business side of my business she does understand people and what they like and don't like.

Kathy served on Integrity Management's board, although there are times I had to beg her to come to the meetings. She found the financial part of the meeting dull, but when we started talking about staffing or marketing she often times came alive with some very good ideas. Since she doesn't understand the business side I usually had to answer basic questions, which seemed to me elementary, but what I learned from this is to stop and rethink about the basics. This requires that I make sure that my decisions make sense on the most basic of levels.

Kathy is just like most entrepreneurs that I counsel. She's hard charging, not very interested in the details, just give her the bottom line and make it simple. This type of accountability keeps me remembering the need for me to keep it simple for clients. I know that if she doesn't understand it, then it's likely that most of my clients may not either.

Another reason that I feel that it is very important that you be accountable to your spouse is the financial accountability that you have. If you are the provider of your household your spouse needs to feel comfortable with what you are doing, and how it affects them. If you are going out and pledging your home as collateral to grow your business, you have an obligation to consult with him or her about your joint assets being jeopardized for the business.

I have counseled with a lot of businessmen that never considered their wife's insight on borrowing decisions. They would often times bully their spouse into signing documents that later the wife may say, if you had listened to me I could have told you that you were destined for failure. Don't make that mistake. If your spouse is not on board with major plans for your business, especially if they affect him or her, then don't do it. It is likely to be God's way of telling you that you are about to make a mistake.

Government

Jesus taught us to render unto Caesar what is Caesar's. Many business people get very angry about what the government requires. Although it is fine in our form of government to be in disagreement with government policies and do our best to change them, it is not fine for us to refuse to comply. Our government has a God appointed purpose of accountability. If there was not a government structure, think of the chaos we would have in this nation.

Since you are part of this nation, you are the government, which means you need to carry your share of the responsibility. If you do not pay all of the taxes that you are legally obligated to pay, then you have shirked your responsibility.

It always angered me when I would review loan requests, and borrowers would try to convince me that I couldn't rely on their tax returns, because they didn't accurately reflect all of their income. This told me that they were not honest and couldn't be trusted. It also told me that I was carrying an additional share of their burden personally, because they weren't paying their fair share of taxes. God does want you to be a good steward and only pay what you are legally obligated to pay, but he doesn't condone illegally circumventing the law.

Many industries also have additional regulations that they are required to meet, including environmental, rate regulations, etc. Government has become more and more a burden to many types of businesses making it very difficult to desire to comply, but yet when you review Romans 13 you will clearly see why God has placed us under government authority and how we are to respond.

Board

Corporations are required to have a board of directors in almost all, if not all states. This is required even if you are a small corporation with one employee. Why do you think that states have required boards of directors for all corporations? I believe that it was originally established to assure that some body of people were responsible for the oversight of the business. I don't believe that it was originally intended to be one of the least thought out parts of business, as it appears to be today in most small businesses.

I know of very few small businesses that have any board members outside of the family or controlling shareholders. It is so typical that the Chairman of the Board will be also the President and CEO, and majority stockholder. Then if that person has not also designated themselves as secretary of the corporation then it will be their spouse, or maybe their attorney. Are there ever any true board meetings? Not usually. Sure they will write up minutes saying they had a meeting, but it never really existed. It's not ever thought of as a guiding force for their future.

Entrepreneurs are so alone in most cases. They are often so self-reliant that it is very difficult for them to recognize that God owns it all, not them. A board of directors, properly developed, can be very valuable. They will provide accountability, oversight, vision, and encouragement. A well-chosen board can save you countless time and money, not to mention giving you friends to turn to for prayer, support, and encouragement when you experience trials.

Someone wise and experienced reminded me that it is easy to put someone on your board, but it can be really difficult to take them off. Choosing a board can be one of your most important steps, if it is done carefully. You should look into choosing people that have a passion for what you are doing, truly care about you and your family, and have excellent judgment.

It is not necessary that they fully understand your business, although I think when possible you should try to get one or two people on the board that do have an understanding of your business. Examine personalities closely. Can you spend the next 30 years following their counsel? Have they been in previous business situations that may be a forerunner of where you are headed? Do they have skills and personalities different from your own? Many times we end up surrounding ourselves with people just like us. If you want to be successful look for people who have strengths where you have weaknesses.

When Integrity Management was formed Gregg Motley and I were going to be equal partners. We both knew from our banking careers that partnerships that are true 50-50 owners rarely last. We also determined that we needed people whom we trusted to guide us. Finally, we knew that we wanted some accountability to our respective churches since this was going to be a ministry. We went to work praying and thinking about how many directors we needed, who should they be, and what should be the ownership structure.

After much prayer and some frustration we developed a group of seven. We developed an ownership structure that gave Gregg and I both 48% of the stock, we had an outside board member from both of our respective churches that each owned 1% of the stock, and we chose a third person from neither of our churches to hold 2% of the stock. We also had both of our wives as board members, although they did not formally hold any stock.

We invested the necessary time to carefully think through all of the possible what-if scenarios that might cause disputes, and developed a majority and super majority voting arrangement so that if either Gregg or I decided to force the other party out at some point it would require all of the other voting shareholders to agree. We built in arbitration procedures by the way that we structured voting rights and stock ownership.

The board members who have supported me in both Integrity Management and Integrity Resource Center have been invaluable. Their Godly counsel, accountability, and business savvy have added significant value. I cannot tell you the number of times that what may have seemed a simple off the cuff statement to them, has become a pearl of wisdom that has saved the business much time and money.

When my wife served on Integrity Management's board I learned that she gave me a higher level of accountability. No matter how well these other directors knew me, they did not know me as well as Kathy. Spouses have the ability to tell us truths that others may not.

Church

I believe that the most overlooked line of authority in our culture today is the church. If you examine the biblical role that the church played in the lives of early church leaders you see a remarkable contrast to what we see today. Most people's lives revolved around the church. Everyone was accountable to the Levites or the appointed church authority. Today it is rare to see submission to the church by its members.

Let me give you an example. I recently had a call from a believer that had experienced a business failure, due to a business partner's supposed purposeful attempt to destroy the business so that he could drive out his partner. Both claimed to be believers. The question to me was "If I can't sue this man because of the scriptural directive against lawsuits against other believers, then how do I resolve this matter biblically?"

As I told this brother, I believe that Jesus gave us an excellent model in Matthew 18 for resolving disputes with brothers in Christ. I recommended that he go to the person first one on one to resolve the difference. Since he claimed to have already tried that, I told him that he needed to go to this person two on one.

I believe that when possible you should go with someone that has authority in the church since we are not to use the world's court system against other believers. So in this case I recommended going to the other parties pastor and asking him to be the second person to go confront this wayward brother.

Most of the times when I make this recommendation people are amazed. Their first reaction is usually, what business is this of the church? In this case, the person that called me had actually already tried this as well, only to find that the attitude of the pastor was that he had no desire to be involved. He didn't think it was his place. What a sad commentary on the perceived role of the church in our lives today.

As business leaders we need to consider what role the church should play in our business. Do you need someone from the church to whom you are accountable? Should you consider how the church could be used to resolve conflicts? Remember in Moses' day all disputes were decided by Moses or his delegates.

For What Are We Accountable

Since we have examined to whom we should be accountable, it makes sense that we should know for what are we accountable. In a nutshell, we are accountable for our thoughts, our actions, our words, and even our omissions.

• Our Thoughts

Jesus really gave us a high standard during the Sermon on the Mount. He discussed the Ten Commandments in a whole new light. He told the masses that day that not only are we accountable for our actions such as anger, murder, adultery, etc. but that we are also accountable for our thoughts. If we wish someone were dead we have murdered him or her in our heart. If we lust after another man's wife we've committed adultery, according to Jesus. What a high standard!

Consider the importance of managing our thoughts. Paul talked about the "renewing of the mind". If our thoughts constantly are thinking about evil, evil actions will follow. Consider the statistics on pornography that we hear on the news occasionally. Almost all sex offenders started out on pornography.

Ted Bundy, before he died, wanted people to know not to take pornography too lightly. He claimed that it led him towards the life of a mass murderer. Although I believe some authors have taken the power of positive thinking too far it certainly is true that our thoughts will eventually have an impact on our actions.

If you are a businessperson that is constantly thinking and scheming about ways to make money, even at the expense of others, you will eventually be found out by your actions.

• Our Actions

If we personally take an action in our business, naturally we are responsible for that action. What if your board recommends that you take an action that turns out to be wrong? Are you responsible? I believe that we are responsible and will be held accountable for everything that we do, but if we do it under the direction of a higher authority they will bear a greater burden in the eyes of the Lord. What if your board directs you to do something that is illegal or against God's law? You will certainly be accountable for disobeying God's law, which includes abiding man's law, unless they violate God's commands.

Business leaders have many opportunities to command someone to perform tasks that may not comply with God's law or even man's law. Are we accountable for actions that someone takes under our direction? Absolutely! If you direct someone to disobey God's law, or man's law, you will pay the consequences. Be careful what directions you give, they may have eternal consequences.

• Our Words

James 3:6 says "The tongue also is a fire, a world of evil among the parts of the body. It corrupts the whole person, sets the whole course of his life on fire, and is itself set on fire by hell." Verse 10 says "Out of the same mouth come praise and cursing. My brothers, this should not be."

There's an old saying that says "a man with few words appears to have great wisdom, while a man with many words confirms that he has none." Gossip, slander, and boasting all are sins that are very difficult to overcome. It is so easy to ruin someone's reputation or to reflect our pride and arrogance through the words that we spew. We are certainly going to be accountable for these words come the judgment day.

There have been times in my own life that I have come face to face with something that I said about someone to later find that it was not true or it was malicious. These statements hurt others and grieve our Lord greatly. When we find ourselves in these sins we need to repent to our Lord. All sin is against the Lord, since everything belongs to him. Repentance is only reflected by action that comes from the heart. If we are truly repentant we should desire to not only make things right with God but also with whomever we have harmed. This can take great courage.

This is an area particularly difficult for me. I have a tough time with keeping from being judgmental of others. The Lord has had to really humble me at times to continually try and teach me lessons about my tongue.

A few years ago I had a boss with whom I had some political difficulties. In the process I got demoted and treated unfairly. I allowed this situation to foster anger and resentment towards this man and soon I found myself speaking poorly of him. In the environment I was in at the time, there were many other people who felt the same way, which only encouraged my sinful behavior.

I carried this anger and resentment for two years before the Lord finally got my attention. As only the Lord can do, he allowed the Holy Spirit to convict me over and over again until I finally brought it to the altar. Unfortunately, that wasn't good enough.

The Bible tells us that if we have a grievance with someone we are to leave our sacrifice at the altar and go make amends. So after two years, I called this man and asked him to forgive me for my anger, resentment, and slander over the past two years. Needless to say he was very surprised by my call. He was very kind about it even though I don't think he fully understood why I bothered to call. That didn't matter, I understood, and so did God, and I came away with a burden lifted that I had carried around for two years.

If you have trouble with your tongue, ask your spouse or a close friend, to help hold you accountable. When you do stumble, repent to the Lord, and if it doesn't make the situation worse, humble yourself and show your repentance by your actions. Go and make amends with that person.

• **Our Omissions**

As difficult as it may seem, we are even accountable for our omissions. If we should have done something that the Lord has asked us to do, but didn't, he is going to hold us accountable. The Lord told Ezekiel in Ezekiel 3 that if he told people God's commandments and warned them of the consequences, and they did not obey, then the Lord would not hold him accountable for those people's actions. But if Ezekiel didn't tell the people, that he witnessed breaking God's commands, of their sin, God said their blood would be on his hands.

This is a daunting responsibility! Do you think *we* have any less responsibility in God's eyes? I think not. There are times in our lives that the Lord will make it clear that he has something he wants us to do. I can tell you from my own experience that if he's asking you to do something it's not usually going to be something easy to do or something with which the world will agree. God will give us a choice. We can choose to ignore his call. If we do there will be a price to pay. It may be a lost opportunity for God's blessing, or it may be God's harsh judgment. Either way God will judge you for your lack of obedience.

Early on, I struggled with how boldly to talk about the foundation of what Integrity Management was about to non-believing business owners. I was referred to a company to do a project for a man that I do not think was a believer. While I was there the Lord made an opening in the conversation for me to give my testimony, but I didn't.

I know in my heart that had I taken that step I would probably still be doing business with that company, whether or not he came to know the Lord from that testimony. Since I was not obedient I am accountable to God for that act of omission. After he did find out what I was about from our client mailings he never would return my call again. I regretfully know that I will stand before God one day with deep sorrow over that missed opportunity.

Recall the story of King Saul and Samuel. Samuel gave Saul very specific instructions from God to wait for Samuel to come before the sacrifice was to be made. Saul made a choice. He decided that his way was better than God's. To Saul it seemed like such a small matter that surely he, as king, should have the ability to decide. As Samuel explained, had there been obedience in the Garden of Eden there would have never been the need for a sacrifice. Likewise, if God asks us to do something, he expects first time obedience, nothing less.

As a business leader we can even be held accountable for our staff's omissions. The Lord tells us to know the condition of our flocks. I have seen many businesses where the entrepreneur is the big picture person who continually overlooks the details. They delegate the administrative affairs and assume that they are getting done without any monitoring whatsoever. Usually in this case they may not find out about their employees' omissions until they get a tax lien or levy. In that case the entrepreneur is responsible, just ask the IRS.

For me I think that it is easier to miss the things that I was supposed to do than it is to recognize when your words or actions did not glorify God. If that is the case for you as well, you might consider a prayer that a friend of mine prays, "Lord, give me directions as big as billboard signs so that I can't miss your will."

How To Begin

Hopefully, by now I've convinced you that you have some things and some people for which and to whom you are accountable. You might be thinking, where do I start, I've been so independent for years, running my own business and avoiding accountability at all costs. **Accountability is something that has to develop into a habit.**

Our culture has brainwashed us into believing that independence is owed to us. Just look at the church in America today. We have taken the Reformation movement to all new heights. We have eliminated any accountability for most of the churches in this nation. The independent churches are missing the Paul-like authority to whom they should be responsible. Even many of the mainline denominations refuse to hold local pastors accountable for fear that someone may require the same of them someday.

For accountability to become a habit you must set some

systems in motion. You first need to determine to whom should you be accountable. Consider the people in your life to whom you should be accountable financially, physically, mentally, and spiritually. Make a list and go to each one of them and request their forgiveness if you have not been accountable and you know that you should have been. Then ask if they would assist you in getting on track.

Give them the authority to be comfortable in rebuking you in the future when they recognize that you have shirked your responsibilities to them. They should be instructed to do this in love but firmly. Also give them authority to go grab another person to speak to you, if they are prayerfully confident that they have rebuked you appropriately, but didn't get your attention.

You will find that most people in our culture are very uncomfortable with rebuking others and will run away from the task if at all possible. Since this is usually the case, you can bet that if they do come to you it probably has gotten pretty bad. One exception to this may be in the urban environment. I am actively involved in an inner city church where I have found that people that have been raised in the urban culture will express their real feelings much quicker than people from the suburbs.

In the suburban church it is so difficult for many people to understand that if you truly love your brother you are willing to make yourself uncomfortable enough to rebuke your brother. I have found it rare that churches will actually do what Matthew 18 calls us to do with a brother that is in perpetual sin.

Two different occasions of adultery surfaced in a former church of mine. The two cases could have been an opportunity for the pastoral staff to sweep one or both under the rug, and I can assure you that would have been a lot more comfortable, but our leadership, praise God, chose to really love these brothers. They followed Matthew 18 to the letter. They tried turning these people back to God one on one.

In one case, that was enough for the individual to repent. He chose to allow the pastor to take it before the entire congregation. He repented publicly, the congregation overwhelmingly accepted his repentance, prayed over him, and developed an accountability system for him to stay on track. His wife and he restored their relationship.

The other party involved in adultery chose to rebel. When approached, he did not desire to change his ways or repent immediately. He was confronted, but without progress. Finally, they brought him before the entire congregation and prayed for him, loved him, developed an accountability group for him, and asked him to repent and turn back to God. He gave it lip service, but then fell away. The pastor publicly revoked this person's membership, while still requiring that the accountability group continue to call and love him.

Many churches have experienced similar events in their church. Oftentimes it is swept under the rug. Eventually the dirt surfaces and the congregation is hurt, people are embarrassed, and the guilty parties leave the church without ever being restored in the fellowship of the rest of the believers. One more walking wounded leaves the church with the feeling that God did not love them, or the body of Christ did not love them. This is not God's will.

After you have spoken with the people on your list about holding you accountable it is good to establish a regular meeting time with one or more of these people to discuss where you are in your life and to reveal any areas in which you need help. Developing an accountability group is very helpful in building relationships so that they know you well enough to confront you when necessary. If someone is not meeting with you regularly it is hard for him or her to feel comfortable in knowing where you are at and what help you might need.

Finally, when you are faced with an issue that makes you uncomfortable or it affects your family, your church, employees, or others around you, then consider seeking God's guidance. This guidance not only comes through prayer, but it also comes from wise counsel from people that know you and what you are about. Talk to your pastor, spouse, friend or all of the above. Don't go it alone, even Jesus surrounded himself with others.

Part II: Management Skills

Nehemiah's Planning Model

"The plans of the diligent lead surely to advantage, but everyone
who is hasty comes surely to poverty." Proverbs 21:5

Over 99% of business owners I surveyed agreed that planning is a valuable tool to be used in business. These same
entrepreneurs were asked how many had done any form of
planning for their business in the last two years. Only 44%
responded affirmatively.

If planning is important, and the Bible even acknowledges
its importance then why do more people not plan? Effective
planning requires knowledge of a planning process that
works. Few entrepreneurs have this knowledge or skill set.

Secondly, so many people get so busy with the urgent
matters in their life that they never find time for the important
matters such as praying, planning, and reflecting on God's
will.

Planning should also be done objectively. This may neces-
sitate hiring assistance, which requires asking for help and
spending money. Two things entrepreneurs dislike.

Another reason planning is not done, especially by entrepreneurs, is that many business leaders are doers not planners.
Most people have a tendency to plan or to do. It's a rare person that is good at both.

To guide you in planning for your business I have summarized a biblical model from the brilliant insights of Nehemiah.

Nehemiah's Model

In 1995 the Lord opened my eyes to a startling discovery,
the book of Nehemiah. This biblical text is a perfect model for
how to fulfill a God sized vision through planning and imple-

mentation. From this biblical blueprint we developed Integrity Resource Center's "Prosperity Plan" to assist businesses in proper planning and ongoing implementation. Let's discuss the steps Nehemiah used to accomplish an incredible feat: rebuilding the wall in record time, and rebuilding the spiritual fabric of his people.

Prayer

Throughout the book of Nehemiah you will find that the cornerstone of Nehemiah's activities was prayer. The amazing thing about Nehemiah is his dedication to prayer and waiting on God's timing to answer the prayers. His story begins with his discovery about the disrepair of Jerusalem.

Being an Israelite passionate for his heritage and people he was greatly grieved by what he heard. Many entrepreneurs might have taken that information, climbed on their camel and headed for the homeland to fix the problem. Others might have said, "That's terrible," and then gone about their business. Not Nehemiah, he began praying and praying and praying.

Nehemiah prayed a remarkable four months about this burden. Then finally the time was right. The Lord showed him favor in the eyes of the king. The timing was so right that Nehemiah not only got permission to leave his important role as cupbearer to go rebuild the wall, but he received the king's blessing, all of the necessary provisions to rebuild the wall, all of the necessary authority to do the job, and all of the necessary provisions to feed himself and his staff.

The king was abundantly generous with Nehemiah and granted all of his requests. This didn't come from Nehemiah's skill and strength, but from God's. Nehemiah's earnest and patient prayers led him to the proper time and approach.

Business leaders, if you want an effective plan for your business don't miss this most important step. Pray! Pray for God's purpose, pray that you clearly understand his purpose, and pray that God will use you in an effective way to accomplish his purpose.

Throughout the entire planning and implementation

process in your business pray at every turn. Pray and then patiently wait for God's timing and leading, not yours. In our society today where waiting at a drive up window longer than three minutes seems unbearable, the hardest thing for most of us to do is to wait on God's timing.

At Integrity Resource Center we provide phone counsel to many business leaders. Occasionally we get the blessing of hearing the end result of our counsel. One day a lady called to give me an update on her previous call to our office. Her husband had been a pastor who had left to go into business for himself. According to his wife the business was struggling, the family was suffering, but most concerning to her was that her husband had stopped praying or seeking the Lord's guidance. Jack from our office grasped the real problem and prayed with this troubled woman specifically that God would help her husband to see the importance of turning back to Him.

The reason for her update was a praise report. She told me that less than an hour after Jack's prayer a customer at her husband's store stopped him to tell him that God wanted him to know that if he wanted his business to succeed he better get back on his knees and seek God. If this wasn't enough the very next day at church another person approached him, and told him they were impressed to instruct him to turn back to God.

This former pastor got the message. He rekindled his relationship with God, with his wife and family, and the last report was that his business was prospering. A simple prayer started the action necessary to bring another one of God's children closer to him.

Assessment

When Nehemiah first arrived in Jerusalem he knew that he couldn't begin work on the wall until he assessed the damage and the current situation. After examining the state of affairs for three days he went out in the evening with his fresh perspective and inspected the wall.

The local people had lived with Jerusalem's disrepair for so long that the heartbreak had become complacency. It took

an objective look from an outsider like Nehemiah to determine the magnitude of the problem. Just like the wall and the
people in Nehemiah's day, many businesses today across the
land are broken, both spiritually and financially. They need an
objective assessment.

The first phase of our "Prosperity Plan" is a diagnostic
assessment. In business you need an objective opinion about
your strengths and weaknesses. Although Nehemiah had different issues to address, the principle remains consistent;
assess your key areas. The key areas to examine in most businesses are financial, operational, sales and marketing, and
management. For nonprofits, fundraising and promotion may
be substituted for sales and marketing.

1. Financial

By looking at the past financial trends of a business, and
their current financial condition objectively, it becomes easier
to determine what strengths should be emphasized and what
weaknesses need to be overcome. We will review eight key
financial factors in Chapter 11 that cover the most important
issues in almost any business. If you are not financially oriented you should probably seek outside counsel to give you an
objective view. Sometimes even if you are financially oriented
you may be too close to the situation to be objective.

2. Operational

In order to produce your product or service it requires
that many operational day-to-day activities take place. If all of
these activities are not being handled properly your customer
suffers, which means you will suffer in the end. I view quality
and productivity as being the two most important factors to
review in the operational side of any business. These areas are
probably the most difficult to assess. They are both subjective
in nature and really boil down to perception, sometimes even
more than reality. Probably the most effective tool to use to
assess quality and productivity is a survey.

If you survey your customers and make it quantifiable you
should be able to get an idea of your customers perceptions of
your quality. They also may provide some insight into your

productivity, but that information will come more directly from surveying your staff. Remember to consider motivations before designing your surveys. If someone feels that they are not speaking anonymously they are likely to tell you what you want to hear rather than what you should hear.

Discussing your strengths and weaknesses with staff and customers will help you to determine your operational short-comings. Summarizing these results is the first step in recognizing the problems that need addressed.

3. Sales and Marketing
If you are in a for profit business, sales is what drives your business. Without sales you have no reason to exist. If you have the right price on your product or service but not enough volume you will fail. It just is as dangerous to have the right amount of volume but the wrong price. If your price is too low you will go broke in a hurry.

Pricing, promotion, product, and positioning are commonly referred to as the four P's of marketing. Promotion includes many aspects of selling, while the other items address primarily marketing issues. Each of these areas need assessed to determine your possible shortcomings. Each should have an underlying principle or strategy driving your approach. If not, it is likely you are reactively addressing issues, rather than building a long term marketing strategy.

For instance, pricing should be a well thought out process that is reviewed on a regular basis to assure you are still in line with your vision and purpose. The beginning part of this process is to take a hard look at your vision for the business. If your vision states that you are a high quality provider of product with the number one market share in your market, but you are pricing the product to compete with Wal-Mart you are likely to fail.

If you have a marketing strategy examine it closely to determine it's viability and how well it is working. In this phase it is important to determine the heart of your sales and marketing strategy. If you don't have a marketing strategy, or a plan written out, you will need one. It will be that all-important anchor when the day-to-day questions come up that may cause you to steer clear of some of the bad decisions that are common when there is no anchor. Once again if you are struggling with determining your strengths and weaknesses in this important area seek counsel.

4. Management

When we assess management we are typically dealing with managing people, money, or time. We have already dealt with money so that leaves time and people. Managing and assessing time requires a close look at your purposes for both the company and for the individual. Time is generally wasted on urgent issues that are not really important to your long-term goals and purposes.

In order to determine if either yourself or your employees are using time effectively, you need to examine the end results. Are the goals being met? If you do not really have goals set then you need to back up and seek God's purpose for the business and for you and each employee.

In order to assess management there are several factors that need to be reviewed. Examine employee turnover, trends in productivity and quality, profitability, and how close are the company and individuals to their goals. You should assess the individuals to assure that their personality traits and skills are suitable for their position.

You should also try to gauge the overall attitudes of the staff and management team. To perform their job at a level of excellence employees need to be well trained, well managed, have a good attitude and desire, and be well suited for their position. If you closely examine each of these in every employee, especially the problem areas, you should be able to identify whether the problem is fixable or not.

In order to determine management's effectiveness you really need to get unbiased feedback from your employees about the people and the systems that are being used to manage. You also need to examine results as compared to expectations of employees and the management team. This can be done with surveys, observation, questions, and review of tangible data.

Goal Setting

It is easy to miss the big picture in the book of Nehemiah. Although the book spends a great deal of time on the rebuilding of the wall, it is obvious from Nehemiah's prayer that both he and God were much more interested in restoring the people spiritually rather than the rebuilding of the wall. The rebuilding of the wall however was important in order to accomplish God's purpose.

In the business world today God is calling His people to come back and renew their covenant with Him. There are broken walls in our business practices that need to be rebuilt; walls like excessive debt, businesses that lack integrity, and businesses that are so steeped in the world's ways of doing business that they have forgotten what God has required.

For a practical plan to be implemented it requires a clear vision and purpose and good long-term goals, as well as short-term goals. Nehemiah knew the vision and purpose was to turn the hearts of the Israelites back to God and restore them to their rightful home. His primary long-term goal to accomplish that vision was to rebuild the wall so that they had a place to move back into that was secure.

Once he had the long term objective clearly in mind it was necessary to sell it to the workers as well as begin breaking it down into bite sized chunks. Nehemiah knew that without a well thought out plan the people would scoff at his idea and it would fail. Needing to be prepared he spent four months praying and fasting about the subject, three days locally examining the situation, and an evening closely examining the damaged wall.

By the time he met with the people he knew what he was faced with and how it needed to be tackled. He solicited support of the leaders, allowed them to form their own teams, provided them with the proper tools and supplies, and then gave them a small enough goal so that all would see immediate success. This immediate success is inspiring to workers so that they begin seeing that the goal can be accomplished.

The team approach was very effective. It is hard to comprehend in our day, with bulldozers and Bobcats and other types of equipment, as to how difficult it must have been to rebuild the wall by hand. The text tells us however that when it was completed in 52 days it scared the nay Sayers, because they recognized only God could have inspired that quick of a rebuilding.

So what can we learn from Nehemiah about goal setting in your business?

1. Pray—pray for wisdom, pray for direction, and pray for the right goals.
2. Keep your vision and purpose in the forefront of your thinking as you set goals.
3. Set long-term goals that will fit with your overall purpose.
4. Break your long-term goals into bite sized chunks, setting yourself short-term goals that are attainable within a reasonable time frame.
5. Develop an accountability method, so that someone holds you to the goals.

Count the Cost

Just when everything seems to be going according to plan all of a sudden there are money problems. Nehemiah was no exception. It appeared that everyone was working together in teams to complete the wall in record breaking time when out of the blue comes the people to complain about their poverty.

This was not just a small money problem. There apparently was a famine, combined with a large debt problem, excessive taxes, and lenders that were less than kind. Could this have been part of God's judgment on their previous activities? It seems interesting that they were experiencing this pain at the same time they were completing something obviously within the Lord's will.

This serious problem required Nehemiah to call a timeout on the important work on the wall. He had to stop and referee between the lenders and the borrowers. He also had to consider how this was affecting his work. In other words, just like Jesus recommended, he had to count the cost before going forward. The workers could not do their duties well if they were hungry and in bondage. Don't you wish you could call a Nehemiah in to convince your lenders to cancel your debts and pay you back the interest?

In business we need to count the cost of the plans we desire to implement. Plans for serious expansion may not be feasible if the business is already strangled with debt. Just like for Nehemiah a plan to get out of bondage needs to be developed before going forward. This requires a budget of what the future needs to look like financially for success to happen.

In planning for the future you need to determine what is the cost of your future plans and ask yourself these hard questions. How will you fund those costs? Will it be with debt or equity? Prudently look ahead and develop a realistic budget that reflects how you are going to go about accomplishing your plans. After it's done review it, and ask yourself those same tough questions again. Could it survive the hard times?

A person, who I will call Judy, called to ask for help. She was trying to finish a home she had contracted to build for a couple. She had been in the construction industry, but had never built a home.

Her problem was that she couldn't pay her lumber supplier, and the house was far from complete. As I queried her to gather facts I asked her about the size of the house. She informed me that it was to be approximately 2,500 square feet. I then asked how much they were paying her to build the house. "$120,000," she responded.

At that point I had to break the bad news to her. You can't build a 2,500 square foot house for $120,000. I went on to ask her how much she had budgeted for the house. The silence was deafening, until finally she mumbled, "Was I supposed to have a budget?"

Without a clear understanding of the financial aspects of your business you cannot succeed long term. It's critical that finances become a priority in your plan for the future.

Action Plans

Nehemiah was a man of action. The balanced approach Nehemiah exhibited is very impressive. He was prayerful, patient, and a visionary, but yet when he had planned appropriately he became a man of action. He was so focused on his task his adversaries couldn't pull him away from his duties, even though they tried countless times. Many people are men or women of action, but they don't plan, or they are planners but they never pull the trigger. Nehemiah gave us an ideal model to be both.

Many times in business, budgets are thrown together and then they are never used appropriately. Without detailed action plans it is unlikely you will achieve your goals. The goal-setting phase is the time for your *overall* objectives to be established. For those goals to be accomplished you need to break them down into small steps. Consider using the SMART method to assure that they are Specific, Measurable, Attainable, Realistic, and Time restricted.

As an example your company goal may be to achieve $1,000,000 in sales next year. The related action plans may be items such as hiring a new salesperson, developing a marketing plan, or developing a new product line.

Bill, a former boss, was a master at leading his staff through developing action plans and holding us accountable to them. Being a self-starter I would usually try to leave, after hearing what he wanted, to go begin on the project. He would stop me and ask what steps I was going to take to complete the task. He would open his calendar and ask, "When will each step be done?" Bill required an estimated completion date before I could leave. On that date you could always count on Bill asking for the resulting report or project. I wasn't pleased with that approach, but it was remarkably effective.

In your business think through the individual steps you are going to take, set yourself a deadline, write it on your calendar, and have someone hold you accountable. If you learn to do this consistently you will be amazed with how much you will accomplish.

Implementation

As I develop plans for businesses the most difficult and frustrating aspect is seeing to it that the plan actually gets implemented. I can hand someone a plan complete with goals, budgets, and well-defined action plans but if they do not actually implement it into their day-to-day activities and follow through it will not bear fruit.

Nehemiah, on the other hand, knew how to implement. After he had mapped out his plan and set his goals, he called together the important leaders of the community and sold his vision, allocated the work, and the work began. Not only did it begin, but it must have been done very efficiently and effectively to have completed it that quickly.

Nehemiah was extremely focused and kept working in spite of adversities. The Bible tells us that even when important rulers called for him to come meet with them he said no. When he feared being attacked, his people were armed with weapons in one hand and continued their work with the other hand. What perseverance!

Once you have your plan for your business be like Nehemiah. Get focused, stay on track, and keep working the plan. Nehemiah led by example, but he also was wise enough to know he needed help, so he rallied the existing leaders and allowed them to develop their own teams to do their section of the work. He did have to pause and assess their progress and adjust problem areas at times but never forgot what they were to accomplish.

If you have trouble implementing, look for someone to hold you accountable. Set specific checkpoints to review your progress with another person that cares enough to hold you to your goals and deadlines.

Follow-up

Nehemiah could have quit after the wall was completed. He could have gone back home victorious, bragging about his accomplishment of building the wall in a record 52 days. The world tells us to quit while you're ahead. Nehemiah knew however that God was not finished with all that he had in mind for Jerusalem. Nehemiah knew that for a plan to be fruitful, a follow-up strategy needed to be developed and implemented. Many people develop a plan for the next year and then stop. What about the following year? Isn't there more to do? Doesn't God have more in store for your business to accomplish than the next year's goals?

After Nehemiah finished the wall he was open for God's leading as to what was next. He knew that God's plan was not about a wall, but about lives. He researched what had happened to all of the Israelites that should have been living in Jerusalem, and worked on bringing them back into the city.

After the people were assembled a great revival broke out as they were convicted by the word of God. Eventually, Nehemiah did have to go back to the king. He wanted to assure that his plan continued as God designed. He chose Godly leaders with wisdom to lead the group. Even with this precaution, the best plans can go bad without some accountability.

When Nehemiah came back to visit the next time he was furious to find all of the sinful activities that had picked back up again. There was no respect for the Sabbath again and even some of the Levites had allowed their family to marry into other neighboring peoples.

The lessons I have learned from these passages are many. A plan is never complete. It needs to be an ongoing process that is constantly monitored and modified. For a plan to be effective there needs to be both wise leaders and accountability. The plan needs to be focused on the eternal results, not the material results. If you only look for the material harvest and set your goals accordingly you will miss God's purpose. His purpose is generally about relationships.

Summary

The book of Nehemiah is a great lesson plan for planning the future of your business. The lessons are new and fresh each time I study this insightful book. The key steps I have developed from the writings of this well-balanced planner and doer are as follows:

1. Assessment—assess the damage. Look for the strengths and weaknesses in your business.
2. Goal Setting—set long-range and short-range goals.
3. Count the Cost—many plans fall apart when consideration is not given to the cost. Develop a budget that is reasonable and stick to it.
4. Action Plans—if you don't develop step-by-step action plans you are unlikely to accomplish your goals. Use the SMART acronym. Goals should be Specific, Measurable, Attainable, Reasonable, and Time Restricted.
5. Implementation—all the plans in the world are no good if not implemented. Take action and implement the plan.
6. Follow-up—planning is never complete. It's an ongoing process that requires constant follow-up and accountability.

Discovering God's Plan

"Many are the plans in a man's heart, but the counsel of the
Lord, it will stand." Proverbs 19:21

At the last bank in which I was working the major stockholder came to me one day and informed me that due to family conflicts he and his sister had decided to sell the bank. If I
was interested in buying it, he said, I should move quickly to
put together an investor group, and make them an offer as
soon as possible. Thus began one of the most exciting and
interesting journeys in my life.

There was so much to do and I had no idea where to
start. So I did the most logical thing for me, I turned to my
Lord. For the next 5-6 months I was on my knees in prayer,
constantly asking the Lord what do I do next, who do I call,
where do I find investors, do I borrow any money, etc. Week
after week the Lord would either challenge me with scriptural
principles He didn't want violated, or He would show me
another miracle that kept things on track.

Throughout the process, the miracles that I witnessed
made me confident that the Lord's will was to bless one of
His faithful children with the opportunity to own a bank. I
even had a passage that I was certain promised me that this
"kingdom" was going to be mine.

Well the end of the story is that God had a plan, but it
wasn't my plan. He had a kingdom, but it was a different
kingdom. Another higher offer came in from a big holding
company, and they accepted it instead. In hindsight, God
actually answered my prayers. My prayer, prior to the opportunity to buy this bank, was that the Lord would begin a healing in the relationship between the brother and sister. The
sale of the bank was the beginning of an ongoing healing in
that relationship.

Towards the end of this quest to buy the bank the Lord started to change my focus, via circumstances, prayer, and scripture, as to what He had in store for me. Doors began to open, and a passion began to build to begin a ministry to the business community using my financial management skills. The Lord set in motion Integrity Management.

So what did I learn from this experience that can help you in discovering God's plan for your business? I learned some key things to do and not to do.

Prayer is vital to finding God's course, and for staying on the right course.

Follow His lead. Don't get out ahead of God. His timing is perfect. He is a proactive God, not reactive like we are often-times.

Test what you think He's asking you to do against scripture.

Never presume to know what God's plan is in entirety.

Since each of these points are critical in determining God's plan let's examine each of these points in more detail.

Prayer

The more I go through life the more I am convinced that nothing significant ever happens without prayer. Prayer is a sign of our submission to God's will, our seeking of God's counsel, and our acknowledgment that He is sovereign. He is the only source of all truth. God wants our fellowship. He loves spending time with us. Many times, however, we spend our prayer time with our laundry list of petitions never taking the time to listen. If God is our true boss, and He's in charge, shouldn't we be listening to His orders for the day rather than giving Him ours? Listening to God takes discipline and patience. It has to become a habit so that you understand what it is that God is trying to communicate to you.

Nehemiah was a great model of how we seek God's plan. After being told about the disrepair of Jerusalem he prayed consistently about it for months. He not only prayed about it, but he also grieved over the situation. Over the course of those months God shaped Nehemiah's vision of how the wall could be repaired. I believe this wisdom came as a direct result of his prayers.

Follow God's Lead

One of the most common traits I see in entrepreneurs is their take-charge attitude. This attitude enables them to get things done, but it also can be a hindrance in doing the right things. Scripture is very clear that God is a proactive God. When we forget that we are called to follow God's lead, rather than the other way around, we are likely to charge off in directions that God does not want for us. Following God's lead means learning patience.

Let's look back at Nehemiah again. He knew that he wanted to rebuild the wall, he even had a well thought out plan as to how he wanted to go about the task, but he faithfully waited patiently on the Lord's timing. He waited until the Lord led the way by preparing the King's heart. When the King finally asked Nehemiah what was troubling him he was strong and courageous in seizing the opportunity that the Lord had given him. If we wait on the Lord patiently and follow his lead he will give us opportunities that we would have never dreamed of ourselves.

Test All Things To Scripture

God gave us a playbook for very good reasons. If we only relied on prayer, and thought that God was leading us to do something, without anything to test it against, we would constantly be driven by emotions that had no solid foundation. If we do however test all things to His word, and we recognize that His word is infallible, then we have a checkpoint to assure that we are on the right path.

The Bible is full of principles as to how we are to run our life. It tells us that we reap what we sow. It also tells us to fulfill God's great commission. If we violate these principles there are consequences. If we are trying to determine God's plan for our business, we can help this process by weeding out the things that scripture tells us are definitely *not* in His plan.

An elder of a church once told me that he was certain that God was leading him to invest in a bar. He explained that he thought it would be a great place to witness to the lost. I was thinking, and should have asked, if you loved your neighbor as yourself would you pour him enough drinks that he was legally drunk and then let him drive home? What kind of witness would you be to the spouse of the alcoholic that you served day in and day out? This elder was not even going to be there day in and day out to have an opportunity to witness. This venture ended up failing and he chose personal bankruptcy. I believe this is an example of people in business that rationalize or forget basic Biblical principles that apply to their decisions.

Never Presume to Know God's Plan in Entirety

I wrongly presumed that God wanted to bless me with a bank. Our self centeredness often times gets us focused on what is God's plan for *us*, when God is concerned about His plan for His people as a whole. Look at Moses; God gave Him a mission to bring His people out of Egypt and to the Promised Land.

It would have been easy for Moses to focus instead on *his* understanding of the plan, and quit after Pharaoh's first refusal. If we learn to take one day at a time, only focusing on God's desire for us for that day, it will be helpful in not letting our own pursuits and purposes to overshadow God's purposes. We still plan and seek to follow God's will, but His will is usually going to be centered on His people, not just us.

Understanding God's Vision for Your Business

Moses had been tending sheep for forty years when God spoke to him through the burning bush. At that encounter God gave Moses a vision. It was a vision for the Israelites, not a vision for Moses as an individual.

When you examine the text in Exodus 3 closely you will find that God told Moses that He was going to bring the Israelites up out of the bondage of Pharaoh, and take them to the Promised Land. Moses' directive was to lead the Israelites out of Egypt.

God did not tell Moses he would lead them into the Promised Land, although it would have been very easy for Moses to assume he was to get that privilege as well. God also left out the part about wandering around the desert for forty years with a bunch of grumbling ingrates. The vision, or revelation, God gave to Moses was clear, concise, and focused on the big picture, with just enough details to assist Moses in knowing what obstacles he was to face.

When we examine Moses' past we find that Moses seemed to have had an earlier passion for freeing the Israelites from bondage, but he went about it in the wrong way. This passion was surely a God given desire.

If you are in business, God owns your business, just as he owns the cattle on a thousand hills. Therefore He must have a purpose for that business that fits in with His overall plan for His people. Does that mean it is something dramatic like leading people out of Egypt? Not necessarily.

Remember, before Moses was called for that daunting challenge, he was also a business leader, a shepherd. For forty years he led a relatively uneventful life of shepherding Jethro's sheep. God didn't reveal for him the ultimate purpose of these forty years, but with 20/20 hindsight it is obvious that it was a time of preparation and training.

For many business owners the vision for their business consists of "making money." God has plenty of money. That is not a vision, but a byproduct of completing God's vision effectively.

If God has given you a vision of your role to play in His kingdom it is important that you discover it, and clarify it, so that you can communicate to others the importance of the vision. Many times there is a vision, but it is deep in the soul, and needs to be uncovered. If after soul searching there is no clear vision for your future it may well be that you are in a season of grooming.

If you are being groomed, your vision should be focused on doing the best work possible in your current vocation. The sooner you shine in your current role, the faster God will be willing to move you into more important roles He may have in store for you. Your current calling, no matter how menial it may seem to you, is important to God. While others may be looking for how important you are, God is interested in how obedient you are, and the heart attitude you reflect in your daily activities.

In order to be clear as to God's vision for your business you first need to determine what his plan is for you personally. God has given you gifts, talents, and skills that He has not given to others. Prayerfully examine your spiritual gifts, your strengths, your weaknesses, your work, and your personal background and interests. Develop a personal mission statement that states what are your primary purposes with your life relative to the roles and responsibilities that you have, such as your family, business, church, etc.

Once you have a clear understanding of what God desires of you personally you should next develop a vision statement for your business. Although I use vision statements, mission statements, and value statements as tools in this book I want to emphasize that I am not as concerned with what you call them, or whether or not you do them in a similar manner. Instead I am concerned with the principles involved in developing these statements. If you do not place before yourself and your staff a vision, there will be no passion and no direction.

You should be able to succinctly state what role your business is to play in God's eternal purpose. Maybe He's wired you for evangelism, or maybe you are a discipler. Whatever it is, He has a method in mind for you to accomplish His purposes. The vision statement will usually be broad enough that you can do business in many different ways and still accomplish His purposes. As an example, the following statement is the vision of Integrity Resource Center.

The vision of Integrity Resource Center, Inc. is to build a comprehensive biblically based resource center that will connect business leaders with the resources and ministries they need to more effectively impact their workplace for Christ.

You'll notice that this vision statement leaves us a lot of room as to how we are going to accomplish this charge.

Hopefully, this will give you some ideas in development of your own vision statement.

The most helpful thing a vision statement provides is that during trials or chaos it helps you to keep your eyes on Jesus. It's too easy to start focusing on profits or cash flow rather than on your vision. As Jesus said in Matthew 6:33, "But seek first his kingdom and his righteousness, and all these things will be given to you as well." This is hard to do if you haven't spent time with Him in awhile. Spend time with God now and determine what vision and purpose he has for your life and for your business.

Developing a Mission Statement

Jane (not her real name) had a successful sod farm business when an outgoing truck salesman convinced her to be a partner with him in a used truck business. She put up the money and handled the administrative affairs; he sold trucks. From the beginning their mission was truck sales, with used parts and truck modifications as their secondary focus. They wanted to provide the workingman an opportunity to have an affordable truck. For 5 years sales skyrocketed. Profits were good. They won awards for their fast growth and they were on top of the world.

Suddenly, it was discovered that the salesman had committed to an overly ambitious fleet purchase and that the business was beginning to hear from several customers about improper and possibly illegal activities in which this salesman was involved. Jane bought him out quickly and terminated all of his relatives as well. Now Jane was forced to determine how to run a truck business that she actually knew very little about. Her oldest son ran the parts department and naturally was the likely candidate from whom to seek advice.

Over the next two years as profits turned to significant losses the business began shifting it's focus to buying salvage parts, with the dream of selling these at a much greater profit margin than they were getting from trucks. Additionally, the commission program for truck sales was changed which demotivated the sales staff.

As I became engaged in this situation it became evident their new mission was the problem. Their original mission had proven successful, but they had chosen to abandon that niche. In spite of my recommendation otherwise, they decided to focus on the salvage parts, and to downsize dramatically the truck sales. They even considered eliminating the truck sales altogether. In very short order this sizeable business dismantled and failed.

This is a dramatic example of what can happen when your mission is not clear, or it gets changed without careful consideration of the customer's needs and desires.

God not only has a purpose for your business, he even has a plan as to how he wants you to fulfill that purpose. If you don't determine which direction God wants you to take to accomplish his purposes, it is likely that you will be tempted with opportunities that are far outside your gifting and God's best. A mission statement is helpful in narrowing the focus as to how you are going to fulfill God's vision.

If you have a board of directors this is a function in which they should be involved. If not, look for someone to help you with this process. You may be too close to the situation to be objective about your personal strengths and capabilities.

God's purpose for your business might be to save the lost. You could do that through a soup kitchen or through a college campus ministry. If you don't narrow down how God wants you to accomplish the goal you may be performing a lot of interesting tasks for which you are not well suited or equipped.

When developing your mission statement first examine your vision. Consider all of the possible ways that you might accomplish that vision. Then consider your strengths, your skills, your past experiences, and your desires. Do not forget to examine what the day-to-day activities would be like.

If you won't enjoy what you have to do day-to-day it won't be long before you are burned out, or you have trouble getting up in the morning. This is one of the biggest mistakes made when people want to become an entrepreneur. They want so badly to own their own business that many people will go into something they know nothing about, nor would they enjoy.

Years ago I convinced myself that I could enjoy and prosper in the car rental business even though I am not mechanically inclined. I hated jump-starting cars in the winter. I despised hassling with cars 100 miles a way that I had to go find, fix, and bring back to the lot. I disliked getting up in the morning, because I wasn't meant to be in the car rental business. Don't make that sort of mistake. It can be miserable.

Make your mission statement broad enough to include all of the possible approaches you may use later in your business to fulfill your vision. Test them, however, against the vision to assure that you can accomplish your vision with those activities.

Our mission statement has been left very broad by design. I am listing it here for an example, but you might want to consider something more specific and more definitive relative to customer service, quality, employee treatment, or other possible issues important to your vision. It still needs to be kept simple and succinct.

Integrity Resource Center's mission is to impact the marketplace for Christ by practicing, teaching, and promoting God's Word to business leaders.

This mission statement is very flexible in regard to the types of activities in which we can participate. We consult, teach, write, and do radio programs, but all with two common themes you will find in our mission statement: teaching God's commands and principles and teaching primarily to business leaders. God will use this flexibility often to move you into things much different than you might have originally imagined, but still within the framework of your mission statement and vision.

Make your mission statement unique to your organization, but within the framework of your vision. Be sure that it is something you will enjoy doing, and what God wants you doing.

Core Values

If you truly desire to prosper in business, developing your businesses' core values is critical. All through scripture God instructs us to obey his commands so that it might go well with us, and that we might prosper. If we desire to please God, and prosper in the process, instilling the right values in your business is the most foundational thing you can do towards success.

A new wave of teaching values is popping up in the workplace. Some companies teach it from a Biblical perspective, many teach it from a worldly perspective, but it all boils down to, if you live out the commands and principles that God's Word teaches, you will do much better than if you don't.

In a values statement you need to determine what core principles and values are the most important to you and to your business. Reviewing the Ten Commandments and Leviticus 19 is an excellent place to start to determine what values you want emphasized in your workplace. Then, with your employees, develop a specific list of which values you desire to be part of your values statement. Work through specific examples with them on what your expectations would be for each value.

Keep your list of values brief. Too many core values will water down the message and the focus. When you have many people on staff to whom you need to convey the message it helps to keep the number of values between 3-5 items. So pick them wisely.

Each business, due to their unique focus, will likely have some values that are more necessary than others. It is important that we teach and honor all of God's commands, but I believe we need to be sensitive to the ones that are in the forefront of what we are trying to accomplish in our specific situation.

There have been various forms of research done on what values employees expect, and what values are common to successful businesses. Some of the top values consistently listed are honesty, mutual trust, truthfulness, servant leadership (putting others first), integrity, giving credit where due, mentoring, empowerment (encouraged to take risks), openness to new ideas, and leading with a clear vision.

After you have determined what you want your business to be known for in the community in the way of values, you need to properly instill these values into your company and your staff. You might be thinking, how can I do that? Maybe you have employees that don't seem to have much in the way of values.

I think our responsibilities as an employer are very similar to our responsibilities as a parent. God told the Israelites in Deuteronomy 6:7-9 how to instill values into their children. "Impress them (commandments) on your children. Talk about them when you sit at home and when you walk along the road, when you lie down and when you get up. Tie them as symbols on your hands and bind them on your foreheads. Write them on the doorframes of your houses and on your gates."

After you have developed your values statement then you must live it. Live it in front of employees, customers, suppliers, everywhere, or otherwise your staff won't buy in and others will soon realize you are rudderless. Talk about your values wherever and whenever possible, giving examples, and rewarding staff when they model the values to others.

Likewise, when someone is violating your company values you must move quickly to lovingly rebuke them and try to restore them to the proper attitude. If it becomes obvious that they are not going to embrace and comply with company values you must properly address the problem, or otherwise the rest of your organization will not believe you are serious about the values.

Don't let this just be a passing fancy. You need to get in the habit of living these values yourself, as well as continually finding creative ways to reemphasize the importance of them to your staff.

Seeking Counsel

"Where there is no guidance, the people fall, but in abundance of counselors there is victory." Proverbs 11:14

Seeking wise counsel is necessary for us to discover God's plan for our businesses. Many realize that there are proverbs about seeking counsel from an abundance of counselors, but how many of us in business really search for help? Very few, according to my experience. I've seen various reasons: I'm afraid to open myself up to scrutiny, I'm the boss, what do I need counselors for, it's no one else's business, they won't understand my business, and on and on.

Yes, seeking counsel does require us to open ourselves up for outsiders to point out areas for improvement, and maybe even point out our flaws. The benefits on the other hand can be incredible.

Let me give you an example. In a previous chapter I told about a business owner who wanted to acquire companies, but one of his directors rebuked him due to his motive being driven by ego. Had there been no accountability structure in place I am certain that this person's fleshly desires would have cost his business great sums of money.

So what type of counselors should we seek? Here are a few guidelines:

1. Seek wise counselors. I believe that God wants us to seek guidance from people with access to God's wisdom. (See Psalms 1) However, I do not believe that God wants us to seek incompetent counsel. There are many believers that may have a like mind, but they do not have the skills you need. Be cautious and prayerful and God will lead.

I once needed to hire a bank consultant. I felt strongly that for this particular situation God wanted me to have Godly counsel, but I didn't know where to turn. After much prayer I finally chose the best-known firm in our area. After about two meetings with this person I was pleased to find out that God had answered my prayer and I didn't even realize it. This person was a believer, and was very skilled.

2. Look for people who have skills and qualities you don't. It has always been fascinating to me that God puts husbands and wives together that have completely opposite gifts and qualities. That is why I am such a big believer in spouses playing an active role in the direction of the business. They may not fully understand your business, but I'm sure they understand you, and they will have better judgment in areas in which you are weak. Likewise, when you are searching for board members, or top management, pick people who are not like you, but rather people that think differently and look at things differently than you do.

3. Select people whom you trust and who have a heart for God. It is easy to put someone on a board, or in a management position, but it's difficult to remove him or her. Be cautious, prayerful, and selective.

Summary

Discovering God's plan for your business is so imperative. Don't pass up the opportunity to get the wisdom from the source of all wisdom, Almighty God. Prayer, seeking wise counsel, and testing your vision and values to scripture will allow you to hear from God. He does have a plan for your business and you can either seek knowledge of His plan, and hear from Him on judgment day "well done, good and faithful servant," or you can go it alone and experience a lot of disappointment and fail God in the process.

CHAPTER EIGHT

The Best Servant of All

"If anyone wants to be first, he must be the very last,
and the servant of all." Mark 9:35

Humility and meekness in a leader is not often found. We have trained people to believe that these are characteristics of weakness. According to many, weak people in business are to be destroyed. How does that line of thinking compare to scripture?

Judges 6-8 tells an interesting story about a meek and humble leader. We're told that the Israelites once again had done evil in the eyes of God, so for seven years he turned them over to the Midianites. Now this was not exactly a pleasant environment for the Israelites. The story reveals that the Midianites were so oppressive that the Israelites had to hide out and live in caves and shelters in the mountains. Not only did they suffer through poor living conditions, but also they were tormented, aggravated, and hungry.

Read what scripture tells us in Judges 6:3-6 "Whenever the Israelites planted their crops, the Midianites, Amalekites and other eastern peoples invaded the country. They camped on the land and ruined the crops all the way to Gaza and did not spare a living thing for Israel, neither sheep nor cattle nor donkeys. They came up with their livestock and their tents like swarms of locusts. It was impossible to count the men and their camels; they invaded the land to ravage it. Midian so impoverished the Israelites that they cried out to the Lord for help."

A military strategist would tell you they had a pretty bleak situation. The Israelites were outnumbered, had poor food supply, very little resources, and a ruthless opponent. Sounds to me like a time if there ever was one to look around and find the meanest, strongest, and most fearless leader you can find. But remember God's ways are not our ways. He picked Gideon.

The story tells us that Gideon was threshing wheat in a winepress when the Lord found him. When the angel of the Lord came to him he told Gideon, "The Lord is with *you*, mighty warrior." Gideon humbly said, "But sir, if the Lord is with *us*, why has all this happened to *us*?" The Lord also told him, "Go in the strength you have and save Israel out of Midian's hand. Am I not sending you?"

I don't know about you, but I would be backpedaling pretty fast if the Lord was giving me that mission. It reminds me of the show Mission Impossible, "Jim, your mission, should you decide to accept it, is to save the world." I find it interesting that Gideon could have made plenty of excuses about *us* not being able to overcome the Midianites, but instead he meekly responded, "But Lord, how can *I* save Israel? My clan is the weakest in Manasseh, and *I* am the least in my family."

To further show us this man's timidity, scripture says that when the Lord told him to tear down his father's altars to other Gods, and replace it with an offering to the one and only true God, he did it at night, because he was afraid of his family and the men of the town.

Does this sound like the typical leader that you or I would choose to lead mission impossible? I think I would have been looking for someone else. Gideon didn't even have the courage to gather support. The Spirit of the Lord had to come upon him to get him to blow the trumpet, rallying the troops to follow him. He was not like most leaders that I see in business. The typical entrepreneur charges ahead now, and asks questions later. Not Gideon, he was very cautious. He still couldn't believe (even though he met the angel of the Lord face to face) that God would choose him to lead the Israelites out of this terrible oppression. Gideon laid out his infamous wool fleece, not once but twice, and asked God to confirm the outcome of the battle.

This story is full of examples of Gideon's servant attitude. Most leaders are constantly striving to grow their power base.

Gideon had 32,000 men that wanted to follow him, but he chose to downsize (with God's guidance) to 300. He could have sent out scouts, but he went himself. He could have sent men into battle before him, but he led the charge. He could have forced his men to execute prisoners, but he did it himself. He could have become king after the victory (the people asked him), but he declined.

What was the result of this humble, meek, and sometimes fearful leader's mission? Mission impossible accomplished with excellence! 300 men conquered the Midianites, the Amalekites, and all the other eastern peoples that had settled in the valley, as thick as locusts. Their camels could no more be counted than the sand on the seashore. This was done with a brilliant strategy that only the Lord could have orchestrated.

Why Should We Become a Servant?

After reflecting on Gideon's situation it is obvious that the Israelites could have ignored Gideon, and continued to be impoverished, or they could have picked the strongest and most bold leader among them, and tried to defeat their enemy. Either way the result would have been disastrous, because it wasn't God's plan. If we become as humble and pure as children, then we can become useable by God in a powerful way. By becoming God's *servant* we can become a leader that God can use in a profound way.

There is something about humility that allows us to listen to God. When we are leading by our own strength we typically are not able to fulfill God's plan, because we aren't likely to be able to discern His plan. If we remember that we are children of God, His servants, then when he gives us directions we will be more likely to listen and follow. Sometimes it won't make sense to us, but that's when we are to step out in faith and do it anyway.

Have you ever had a boss that gave you a task to do without any explanation about how it fits into the company's big picture? If you are like me, it probably was sometimes difficult to do, because you could make all kinds of excuses and reasons why it's not important, or why you don't understand why you have to do it their way. Let me give you an example.

When I started a car rental agency years ago, I went to a bank to get a SBA loan for the business. I knew what amount and terms I thought I needed, and how I wanted it done. I had a friend that was the loan officer who diligently fought the battles with his loan committee to get the loan approved. He was turned down once or twice, but persevered until finally he got an approval, subject to one major caveat. The wise, old chief lending officer for the bank suspected that I was undercapitalized, and that things wouldn't go as I had planned, so he made the loan proceeds only available to purchase cars. The bank would only finance 75% of the actual cost of the cars, and none of the loan proceeds could be used for working capital, which is the nice term for operating losses.

At the time, the loan officer thought this stipulation was overkill, and I certainly thought so, but it was the only way I could get the loan approved, so I accepted the condition. A year later, although I wouldn't have admitted it at the time, I learned what great wisdom this was, not only for the bank but also for me. That condition saved me from bankruptcy.

When I ran out of money and needed more cash, I wasn't able to borrow on my loan unless I was buying a car. That provision made it necessary that I stop and review the progress of the business. I sought wise counsel that advised me that if I held on too long to the business, that I would surely go broke. I ended up deciding to liquidate the business. I was able to pay off the bank and my other creditors. Had that stopgap not been in the loan requirements, I know I would have proceeded for another 3-6 months right into bankruptcy. I later worked for that wise old man and learned to respect his abilities greatly.

God is like that wise old lender, he knows where we are headed, he knows why you need to do the things he's asking you to do, even when it doesn't make sense. He also knows that he can't always disclose to us why. Sometimes it's because we are stubborn, and we won't understand until we've learned the hard way. Other times it's because we are not strong enough to know the future.

If God had told my wife that he was going to put her through the trial of breast cancer in order to minister to dozens of women later, I guarantee you she would have done everything in her power to prevent it from happening.

So why should we be a servant leader? Because God has asked us to be humble and obedient. He is the ultimate wise old lender. I've heard it said that there are only two things in life we have to remember. That God's in charge, and I'm not God!

Jesus told us that what we do unto the lesser of these (his children) we do unto him. A great approach to applying this principle is to constantly ask yourself, what would Jesus do?

Who Should We Serve?

In business, most people state that they are in business to serve the customer. Is the customer the only one we are to serve? I think not. Jesus taught that we are to serve our neighbor; his definition of neighbor was a whole lot broader than what, often times, I care to remember. It includes everyone around us. In a business, that means our customers, suppliers, employees, bosses, board of directors, prospects, creditors, and anyone else that we stumble across. That is a hard thing to implement when your customer is complaining, an employee just cost you a large job, or a supplier just cut you off.

• Employees

I think that as employers our first obligation is to our employees. The relationship between an employer and employee is similar in many ways to that of a father-child relationship. God has entrusted that person to us, and we are called to be good stewards of the human resources, as well as the financial resources. If you go along with the belief that the business is similar to a family in our responsibilities then 1 Timothy 5:8 can be very convicting when it says "If anyone does not provide for his immediate family, he has denied the faith and is worse than an unbeliever."

Nothing could be more humbling than gathering our

employees and serving them to the point of taking off their
shoes and washing their feet as Jesus did the disciples. In
today's culture, that would be similar to giving your lowest
paid employee the keys to the company car, the country club
membership, and the biggest office.

• Customers

From a practical matter customers need to be served and
served well, if we desire our business to prosper. We have
given a great deal of lip service in this country in the last several years about customer service, total quality management,
etc. but have been very poor on implementation. As smaller
businesses have been gobbled up by the large ones customer
service has suffered. Sure the big corporations give it lip service because they know that Wall Street likes to hear the latest buzz words, but few actually care.

It is hard enough for a small business to stay close enough
to their customers to show that they truly care, let alone a
large corporation that is so far removed from the front line
customer service representatives. I actually chaired a quality
service task force for a Fortune 500 company at one time. I
quickly learned that management wanted results that they
could point to for display to shareholders, but only if they
didn't have to invest any time or energy in it.

The most commonly cited reason for failure of quality service is lack of buy-in from senior management. People only do
what they actually see is important to their superiors. If mid-
dle management knows that senior management isn't serious,
what message do you think they will convey to staff?

A true servant attitude towards customers will only come
from heart-felt concern from front line employees. Heart-felt
concern only comes from a system that truly recognizes,
rewards, and encourages that sort of attitude. Businesses that
take this seriously sell their customer service vision to their
employees from the very first day. Then they sell it again the
second day, and every day thereafter, by rewarding and
encouraging the employees that actually demonstrate it to the
customers and by eliminating the people that don't.

• Board

Any business that has an established board of directors has an obligation to serve that board. As servant leaders, however, the board should also recognize their obligation to serve the staff of the business.

There is fiduciary obligation that business leaders have to their shareholders and board of directors. The board is responsible for determining the strategic direction of the business, and the staff is obligated to carry it out.

Many CEO corruptions have a common theme. The CEO's do not serve their board, instead they manipulate and hand pick board members who rubber stamp their desires. This lack of humility, and the resulting pride, has led to the downfall of many leaders and their businesses. A wise leader humbles himself to a skilled board and serves them well.

• Suppliers and Creditors

According to the Bible, the borrower is servant to the lender. This is one of the few areas where business owners truly serve, and I can tell you from a lender's perspective that it is rarely cheerfully. Usually their service takes place out of requirements that the lender places on them, either to get the loan, or to keep it from being called. One of the first practical rules I learned as a lender was to never give loan proceeds to a borrower, until they had provided you with all of the information and signed all the documents. It was amazing to see that after the money was disbursed it was almost impossible to get documents signed or additional information.

The Lord calls us to serve cheerfully as we are serving him. This means that we need to be cooperative to suppliers and creditors, supplying them with whatever they might need, especially open communication about your circumstances.

One of the biggest issues of conflict in vendor and creditor relationships is lack of communication. It is the norm, rather than the exception, that if a business can not meet timelines to pay, or required disclosures, that most businesses will just ignore it and hope it goes away, rather than calling and communicating to the vendor their circumstances.

Unfortunately, my business had an opportunity to communicate with a vendor in that manner. I had been working on a bankruptcy case that needed court approval before the client could legally pay me. The client's attorney was to have filed the appropriate affidavit, and had indicated to me that he had. After two and a half months I found out that the attorney had never filed the appropriate papers and I had accumulated four months worth of invoices unpaid. I had a bill due with a vendor with no means to pay.

On the day the bill was due I called the vendor to let them know my circumstance, my intentions to pay as soon as possible, and an expected time frame that I hoped to resolve the matter. The other end of the phone was quiet for a moment before this lady said, "You mean your bill is only due today and you're calling to tell me you can't pay yet." I told her that was correct. She said, "We don't ever have anyone calling to tell us they can't pay, especially not calling this soon. I'm just thrilled you called. We are more than willing to work with you until your money comes in."

I believe this is the type of response that most companies would receive from their vendors, if they would only communicate their situation in an honest and forthright manner. Many people can find it in them to serve customers cheerfully, the real witness comes from the people who can serve creditors cheerfully.

How Do We Serve?

Out of the previous list of people we are to serve in business I believe the hardest group to serve for most people are their employees. Employees are subordinate to the owner, because that is who pays them. This can allow ego to rise up in the owner, which can prevent the humbleness necessary in our spirit to properly serve.

Let's look at the model we have been given for servant leadership, Jesus Christ. He had disciples, they followed him, but yet he was always willing to serve them. Probably the most humbling job anyone could perform in Jesus' day was to wash the feet of the people coming in from the dusty road.

But on Jesus' last day, before his crucifixion, he is stripping down to a towel, and washing the dusty feet of the disciples given to him by God.

If it was my last day on earth and I knew it, as Jesus did, I would have probably used guilt to get the disciples to take care of my every desire, rather than humbling myself to serve them in such a degrading way. Jesus left us the example with the words "No servant is greater than his master" meaning that Jesus is God incarnate and we are his servants. Since we are not greater than Jesus, our master, we are to serve others just as Jesus served the disciples that night.

So how can we use this in a practical application to serve our employees? Look around for the tasks least liked in your business. Go and work beside your staff in that role for a day. You will gain more respect and hard work from your employees than 10,000 memos would ever get you.

I once worked for a bank president that I remember took one day to wash employees' cars. There wasn't a special event or any particular reason. He just told the employees to bring their cars around and he would spend the day washing them. It may sound foolish to some, but that act, coupled with his overall servant attitude on a regular basis, built a loyalty that has paid great dividends. He later went to be president of a new bank. He had his pick of any employees he wanted to staff the new bank, because of that loyalty.

Constantly reminding yourself that you are working for God will help to remind you to have a servant's heart. God's work is about relationships. If you begin roaming around your workplace, taking time to visit and getting to know your employees, you will be amazed at the things you learn, the opportunities the Lord will open before you to evangelize or disciple, and the loyalty and respect you will build.

It's easy to rationalize that your time is so valuable in dollars and cents that you can't afford to take time to visit your employees. When you realize that a little time and concern for your staff will greatly improve their productivity, you will begin to see fruit not only financially, but spiritually also.

I challenge you to ignore pride and ego, to ignore conventional organization charts, and begin leaving an example to your staff of being a true servant leader. A true servant leader performs service with a cheerful attitude. Who knows, you may find yourself mentoring an upcoming great leader that will impact millions.

People: The Greatest Asset

"Be sure you know the condition of your flocks, give careful
attention to your herds; for riches do not endure forever,
and a crown is not secure for all generations." Proverbs 27:23-24

Since relationships are so important to God it is obvious
that the greatest resource God gives us as business owners are
the people under our care. In many businesses however this is
the most overlooked resource. They tend to value the financial results much more than the people whose lives their decisions affect.

During the beginning of the massive downsizing in corporate America a Saturday Night Live skit was about a TV talk
show program that had three or four CEO's of major corporations on the show discussing their staffing levels. Each CEO
was portrayed as having a very large ego. As the discussion
progressed they began challenging each other on how many
people they were going to lay off. It started looking like a
poker game with one saying we're going to downsize 200,000
jobs and the next one saying well I can top that, I'll terminate
300,000.

To the employees that have lost their jobs this skit probably seemed real. Most downsizings show little concern about
valuing the employee as a person, or who will do the work
once they are gone. Someone in the penthouse office says
let's let several thousand people go, without knowing whether
or not it might damage productivity or families' lives.

Within the context of being a good steward of your business, it is important to recognize your responsibility as a shepherd over the flock God has entrusted to you. This necessi-
tates that you examine your human resource practices. Is the
golden rule being maintained in your relationship with your
employees? Are you truly doing to them, as you would want

to have them doing unto you? People that work for you can make or break your business faster than anything else. Many of the problems in managing people come directly from poor communication. Each phase of the employee process needs to be clearly communicated, from interviewing all the way to firing.

Interviewing

When you begin the process of needing help in your business don't make the mistake of charging into it so fast that you end up with a bigger problem than you were trying to solve. Begin by asking yourself some very thoughtful and important questions.

1. Do you really need to hire someone, or is there another, less costly way to accomplish the goal?

2. Could you outsource this job instead of adding what usually becomes permanent staff?

3. Are you certain that your current need is not seasonal in nature versus a permanent need?

4. What specifically do you need? Does it need to be part time or full time?

5. What skills are needed to fit the job?

6. What type of personality traits do you need to fit your current team of people and to fit the type of job?

7. What is the going rate of pay for this type of position? What can you afford to pay?

8. How does pay relate to the bottom line productivity you hope to achieve by hiring this person?

9. Can you make the pay structure variable in nature in case it doesn't turn out as well as you hope?

10. Would an incentive pay structure be more effective?

11. What personal values, characteristics, lifestyles do you desire of this employee or that you will not accept?

In order to be a good steward of your time, as well as respecting the people's time that you interview, it is important that all of the above questions are thought out in advance and a plan developed to assure that you ask questions that are legal and appropriate.

Next, develop a job description; it will save you a lot of time and trouble in searching for the right skills. A job description should reflect the goals of the position and a detailed list of the daily responsibilities and duties to be performed. Identifying the skills and necessary education on the job description will also assist you in the screening process.

Another thing that I believe is very valuable for serious candidates is a personality assessment. Many people do not work out in a job for reasons other than skills. If you have the right skills, but your personality is wrong for that type of position it causes much frustration for you as well as the employee. If you are trying to hire for a particular position, and you know someone who performs that type of job very effectively somewhere else, consider getting a personality profile from him or her as a guide for what kind of person you need to hire.

In the process of trying to hire an administrative assistant/office manager I drafted a job description and thought about what kind of person I needed. I kept thinking how much I wish I could hire someone just like one of my former administrative assistants. So I called her, knowing that she was happy where she's at, and asked her if she would mind completing one of Crown Financial Ministries personality profiles. This profile gave me a good benchmark to use in trying to select someone to fill the job.

There are many different types of these profiles available. They are great for understanding how effective that person will be in your environment. They still have to have the necessary skills, but I would rather have someone who possesses the personality traits necessary and be willing and able to learn the skills, than to have someone with good skills but who would be unhappy in that environment.

These assessments are also very useful in rounding out your team as well. It's human nature to appreciate people who think like us. If your entire team begins to look and think like clones of you it will be difficult to find a fresh perspective to the problems you face. Other personalities and thinking styles are very helpful in drawing the right conclusions in business.

Spend the time and the money to pick the right person for the job. Hasty decisions have resulted in countless thousands of dollars wasted in many businesses.

Hiring

Once you have determined what duties need to be performed, what kind of person you need to perform those duties, and have interviewed candidates, it is time to select and hire the right person. Many people are hired based on the chemistry they had with the interviewer. Although it is important that there be a peace about whom you are hiring you shouldn't base your entire decision on that factor.

In Joshua 9, the Israelites learned the lesson of being diligent in their decisions by both seeking God's counsel, and doing the necessary legwork, to make the right decision. You can ask all the right questions and do the necessary due diligence, and still be deceived if you do not seek the Lord's counsel. On the other hand, if you presume that your peaceful feelings are from the Lord, and don't do the proper due diligence you are likely to find that you misread God's leading.

Selecting the right person should be a process of examining carefully their skills as compared to the job description, their personality traits as they relate to the environment, job, and team, and seeking God's counsel. Checking references is highly recommended to assure that what they have told you is truthful and to gain any further insight into strengths and weaknesses.

Unfortunately, in our litigious society most companies today avoid giving you any information about their past employees except for dates of employment. If you can get a supervisor's name you might find out more. If you reach someone willing to talk it is important that you have thought out what questions you need answered. Try and get as much objective data as possible rather than subjective. You might consider asking questions like "On a scale of 1 to 5 how would you rate them in..." Ask questions that relate to skills and personality traits needed for the position.

I had a client that hired people primarily from his church

without much regard as to their skills or personality characteristics for the job. He ended up with a sales type running the accounting department, and a detailed person as his sales manager. As you might expect the accounting department turned into a disaster, with very little filing done and no records being kept, while the sales department was bogged down with a great deal of paperwork. After it was decided that these two people's jobs be switched there was much less tension in both locations and things suddenly got more organized and effective than they had been.

A question asked by many business owners is should I only hire Christians? I think that this is an issue that should be thought out very carefully. There are occasions when you definitely should only hire believers, such as a church, parachurch, or other forms of ministry. However, if all businesses only hired Christians, they would primarily only be ministering to each other with no effective evangelism going on in the workplace. I know several business owners that get great joy out of the evangelism that they are able to do right in their own workplace.

It is important that you prayerfully consider what God desires to do through your business. If he wants to use your business to witness to the staff, then there's your answer. If on the other hand you feel that you are called to "feed his sheep," then you might be a discipler that is better served nurturing young believers in the faith. Whichever you feel called to do remember that God desires excellence in the workplace. Be a light on the hill, if you have incompetent Christians at work your light will be dim.

Compensation

Once you have determined whom you would like to hire, compensation is usually the next big hurdle. Compensation in small businesses needs to be given much thought. It is common to find out how much the person you want was making in their last job, give them a small raise, and hire them. This approach is full of pitfalls. By taking this approach a few things can, and oftentimes does, happen that may cause you significant problems. Let me give you an example.

Suppose you have hired a bookkeeper for your business. Jane, a 50-year-old female was well qualified and seemed to have the skills and personality to fit well within your company. She had only been making $8 an hour at her last job. So you hired her at $8.75 an hour. She does an excellent job for you and your business is growing rapidly.

Six months later it is time to hire another person. You still need basically the same skills and personality fit for the new hire. This time you don't have as many applicants, the job market has gotten tighter, and the quality of applicants doesn't seem as good.

Finally, you find a young man, Bob, who has similar skills and personality as the first hire, but not quite as much experience. You decide that this is the best you are going to get, and you need to fill the position quickly, so you begin to discuss salary. You are dismayed to find that at his last job Bob was making $10 an hour and has said that he won't make a change for less than $11.50. Out of desperation you go ahead and hire him.

The next two years go by with both people doing a good job. Their performance reviews are basically the same with Jane slightly better due to her experience. They have each been given 5% raises for each of the last two years.

Suddenly, the head of your bookkeeping department resigns, and you are a strong believer in promoting from within. After discussions with both likely candidates you decide to promote Jane and generously give her a 15% raise. You think that the problems have all been solved and everything will be great until Jane comes into your office the following week hopping mad.

Jane has just realized after reviewing her department's payroll records that she is only making $11 an hour while Bob, who now reports to Jane, is making $12.68 an hour. Jane demands to know why she has been treated so poorly when she knows that her performance reviews have been better than Bob's the last two years, but yet Bob has consistently been paid more. She raises the ever-fearful prospect of an age discrimination suit and leaves your office in a huff.

Not only is Jane mad but also Bob is not happy that he

was passed over for the promotion, so suddenly your whole bookkeeping department is in chaos. "How did I get into this mess," you ask yourself.

This scenario is not uncommon in business. An added problem is that you can take the typical annual raise for cost of living, etc. out five years or more, and realize that you are now paying your existing people significantly more than what you may be able to hire the same skills for in the marketplace. So what are the solutions?

We have developed a pay system in corporate America that needs to be revisited. In order for businesses to survive, remain competitive, and adhere to the golden rule of doing unto others as you would want them to do unto you, we need to develop a pay system that rewards people for their skill level and for their part in the business' productivity and profitability.

Bonuses and cost of living raises that are not tied to performance or enhanced skills do almost nothing for motivation and further development of our staff's potential, not to mention profits. Cost of living raises actually perpetuate the need for further cost of living raises. The same principle as compound interest works to increase wages over time beyond what the going rate in the market is for that skill.

I recommend making pay as variable as possible, tying it to the overall performance of the business, with raises being given only for improved skills that add to the productivity of the business. To those that are stuck in the traditional methods, this may strike fear in their heart.

Pay for performance however will greatly reward your employees and your business as your staff finds that they are able to give themselves a raise simply by working harder and more effectively. If they focus on the goals that will actually improve the profitability and productivity of the business the business will prosper and they will share more in the gain.

This requires a degree of disclosure on the business owner's part, which may be uncomfortable for many. Open book management is a topic discussed often today as if it is a totally new concept. But if you review the Bible and think about it you'll recognize that most businesses during Biblical times were farm related. If you were a hired farm hand you could see the harvest. It was pretty easy to determine how much grain was harvested and what it was worth.

Paul said in 1 Corinthians 9:7-10 "Who serves as a soldier at his own expense? Who plants a vineyard and does not eat of its grapes? Who tends a flock and does not drink of the milk? Do I say this merely from a human point of view? Doesn't the Law say the same thing? For it is written in the Law of Moses: 'Do not muzzle an ox while it is treading out the grain.' Is it about oxen that God is concerned? Surely he says this for us, doesn't he? Yes, this was written for us, because when the plowman plows and the thresher threshes, they ought to do so in the hope of sharing in the harvest."

Proverbs 16:26 teaches, "A worker's appetite works for him, for his hunger urges him on." Be creative; develop a gain sharing system or some sort of incentive compensation system that allows your staff to share in the harvest. You can't do all the work yourself. If you allow the staff to share in the profits they will take ownership of their part in your business and will be much more conscientious and productive. With these sorts of systems you will lose the people that only want a wage and would prefer to be slothful. But the ones that are looking for recognition for their hard work will stay and be more productive and happier.

A biblical view of someone who truly knew the benefits of sharing the harvest was Joseph. After the famine had wiped out all of the Egyptians, except for the Pharaoh's possessions, all Egyptian land was sold to Pharaoh at rock bottom prices. Joseph purchased the land on Pharaoh's behalf, but he was extremely generous considering he now owned the land and the people were his servants.

Joseph asked that they pay only 20% of the harvest to Pharaoh, even though it was his land. He allowed the original sharecroppers to keep 80% to provide for their families and to provide for the seed for next years crop. They were overjoyed that he was so kind. They knew that he could have easily reversed the split and still be considered fair.

Did Pharaoh suffer in this deal? I don't think so. He still owned the land, so he could do anything he wanted with it later. He was also creating wealth by allowing the people to prosper from the work of their hands. They were sure to do a better job of managing Pharaoh's property and were making themselves potential buyers for the land in the future should Pharaoh decide to sell.

A biblical discussion on compensation cannot overlook minimum pay requirements. Deuteronomy 24:14 tells us, "You shall not oppress a hired servant who is poor and needy, whether he is one of your countrymen or one of your aliens who is in your land in your towns." Many businesses profit on the backs of their employees by paying the absolute minimum they can.

If we are good shepherds over the staff the Lord has blessed us to manage we should care for their well-being. A living wage should be paid to everyone. If you cannot afford to pay a living wage, then maybe you have the wrong person or a position that is not viable for the long term.

Training

Many businesses, especially smaller companies, overlook the importance of training. Too many times we hire a new employee expecting that they are ready to hit the ground running. We hand them a project without much direction, check back with them later, only to be disappointed that either the project is not done or it's done very poorly. If we truly love and care for our employees we will desire them to succeed. Success doesn't just happen via osmosis. These people need training on both your companies' way of doing things and on the skills necessary for them to complete the given tasks.

The first training necessary for a new hire should be on the company culture, values, and policies. If you want this new hire to be an ambassador for your company, then it is imperative that they fully understand what your company is about.

They need to know about your company's products and services, their part in producing these products and services, how you make money to stay in business, what values are important to you, what will be expected of them, what company policies there are that will impact them, and the basic do's and don'ts about your operation. This seems so basic, but very few businesses truly do a good job in this area. Part of it is because many businesses have not developed the answers to these basic questions.

Once you have trained your new employees on these important matters your training job is not over. You want these people, who are so important to the future success of your business, to be as equipped as possible to not only do their job, but to improve and be developed into leaders for the future.

Training dollars do not usually show immediate bottom line results and therefore it is oftentimes difficult for entrepreneurs to turn loose money for this purpose. Study upon study has shown, however, that companies that do pay for added training get more than their investment returned in increased productivity.

Does this mean that you just turn your people loose to go to any seminar that strikes their fancy? No, this would be poor stewardship. Each individual has different strengths and giftings. Employees, either in their performance review or at some other time, should have a development plan for his or her future growth. Identify what you think they are capable of in the future and compare this to their thoughts.

Examine the needs of the company in the future and jointly work out a plan as to how you are going to assist each employee to reach their full potential. Identify specific training possibilities for them to achieve those goals, and budget time and money accordingly.

Reviewing and Rewarding

Performance reviews are essential for there to be open communication between employees and employers. This needs to be a formalized process so that there is actually time invested in doing it properly.

I once was hired to manage a lending department for a regional bank. When I arrived I found that there had not been any structure, no lending policies, no personnel policies, or anything that resembled order. I had several employees assigned to me that had worked in this environment for quite some time.

When I first implemented performance reviews I found that the employees believed that they had been getting reviews in the past and that this was nothing new. As I probed further about their past reviews I found that basically all of them once a year would be called into the President's office, told that they had done a good job, whether or not that was true, and given their annual raise.

It was difficult at first to convince this group that in order for them to reach their full potential their review needed to be more in depth. One young loan officer was crushed after her first review as I explained several shortcomings that were hampering her career.

She was mad at first, because she had always had good reviews in the past, and she was not prepared to hear any negatives. I assured her my hope was to develop her potential by emphasizing her strengths and working to correct her weaknesses. After many months I was pleased that some of the areas we had addressed started to improve and she became a more valued employee. She grew to appreciate that had someone been forthright with her previously she could have developed much sooner into a better lender.

Just like developing a plan for your business, performance reviews are a tool to help develop a plan for each employee. You should assess their past performance, identify their strengths and weaknesses, and map out a plan for where they are going. I have always appreciated the bosses that cared enough for me that they wanted me to succeed even if that meant my next step was out of that job or even that company. The Biblical approach to managing people is to desire success for your staff in spite of your own self-interests.

It is preferred to have a developed format to follow when doing reviews. This assures you are consistent in how you handle reviews with each employee, and makes sure all necessary areas are addressed. To do an effective review use good communication skills throughout the year.

This requires documentation throughout the year of

things that need to be mentioned. Avoid surprises. No one likes going into a review with a boss that brings up problems that happened months ago. If throughout the year there are problems, address them immediately. Just like it doesn't do much good to punish your child the day after poor behavior, it also doesn't work to punish employees substantially after the fact. This kind of practice is not fair to them.

Before giving reviews ask yourself how you would react to each bit of news that you intend to share. Would it hurt, send joy, or make you disappointed. Anticipate the reactions and be prepared to be empathetic. You owe it to each person to dedicate enough time to this process to do it right, both on the front end of preparing the review, as well as setting aside quiet time for the review without interruptions. Remember, God is more concerned about that person, and the relationship you have with them, than he is about the to-do list you have on your desk.

Most businesses have set a standard of giving raises during the performance review. Although I believe rewards should be given, along with recognition of someone's performance, I think we have caused a great deal of harm to business, and to employees in the manner it has been done in times past.

I worked for a major corporation that gave lots of lip service to the fact that they valued their employees, and would reward them based on performance. That year I had outperformed my peers significantly, as was noted in my review. When it came time for my raise I was told I had done such a good job I was going to receive a raise at the top of the range allowed that year, a whopping 5%. At my request I was told 3% was the low end of the range.

I was upset. "You mean had I not worked hard all year, and just laid back and relaxed," I said, "like many of my peers, I would have gotten a 3% raise?" For all my hard work, and significant bottom line improvement for the company, it only gained me an additional 2%.

If we structure our pay and rewards relative to performance you will have some who will not receive any increase, which will also allow you more flexibility for the top performers. A cost of living type increase is not paying for performance. Pay should relate somehow to the employees actual contribution to the business.

In rewarding employees most management teams typically focus on compensation alone. Surveys reveal that although management usually ranks compensation as the highest factor in what motivates employees, the employees rank it much farther down the list. They would much prefer recognition for their accomplishments. This can be done in cheaper and more creative ways.

Basic communication skills end up being the best way to reward people. If they are doing a good job, let them know it then, not later. If they've gone the extra mile for you or your customers consider ways to publicly recognize them. I think the philosophy of praising in public and disciplining in private makes for the best relationships.

Award ceremonies, cash bonuses on the spot, employee of the month, team rewards, etc. are all ways to boost morale, productivity, and loyalty. In order to use periodic recognition and rewards effectively it is important to develop a system. It's too easy to get lost in the day-to-day activities and forget to look for these opportunities. Many people start a program and then never follow through. Schedule time for yourself and your managers to review progress towards recognizing employees.

Discipline

Disciplining employees is a difficult issue for many managers. Either they are afraid to resolve an issue, or they react abruptly to a situation without thought. Both of these approaches are damaging to the employer-employee relationship. I witnessed the fallout of one of these type situations.

A bank president I knew had an employee that every year had been given the typical "good job" review and a pay raise. Any ongoing problems were never discussed. This employee had reportedly been notorious for treating customers rudely, which was a real irritation to the bank president. Finally, one day the bank president walked by as this employee was verbally abusing a customer. The president lost control. He fired the man on the spot.

This man filed an age discrimination suit. Even though the jury knew the reason he was fired had nothing to do with age, especially since a much older female replaced him, a jury awarded him a significant amount of money.

If you need to discipline an employee remember the golden rule, and treat them as you would want to be treated. Here are some other points to remember:

A. Do it promptly.

B. Do it gently but firmly.

C. Make sure that you have facts, not rumors, when you discuss the issues.

D. Have a definitive action plan as to future expectations for the employee.

E. Give them all of the assistance and support you can to accomplish the stated goal.

F. Give them ample time to work on correcting the problem, and a very clear idea of the consequences if they don't comply.

G. Assure them you desire to restore them to be a valuable employee.

If you dismiss a problem rather than address it immediately, the other employees may lose respect for you as a manager. Another common mistake is when a manager has a problem with an employee, rather than go directly to that person, they call a staff meeting and announce the problem in a generic sense and ask for it to stop. The difficulty with this approach is that everyone at the meeting usually knows who you are talking about, and they are angry to be reprimanded for something in which they had no part. The person who needs to be listening usually either rationalizes that you must be talking about someone else, or they view the meeting as the chicken way out, so they test you even more to see if you have the courage to confront the problem.

To summarize, in disciplining employees you will have greater success if you treat others as you would want to be treated. Show concern for your people, and communicate openly, and you will have dedicated employees.

Dismissing

Dismissing an employee hurts. If you value and respect people, letting someone go will be one of the toughest jobs you will ever perform. Leave them with dignity. The entire process should be well thought out and handled delicately.

There are proactive approaches to minimize the necessity for having to dismiss an employee. Good hiring practices will prevent a lot of pain. Don't hire someone unless the work can't be done any other way. Provide adequate training, coaching, and structure to assure they have the tools to succeed.

Even when you are proactive there will be times when dismissal is warranted; either you make a mistake in hiring, or circumstances change either in your business or with the individual. After you have exhausted the discipline process, and it becomes evident that things are not going to change, then you should begin planning for their dismissal.

Dismissal for performance reasons should only come after you have attempted to restore the person in a productive way. Dismissal for non-performance reasons, such as a need to cut staff due to economic reasons, should be done cautiously and only as a last resort. Look for creative ways to accomplish your staffing goals. I have seen job sharing, switching full time staff to part time, across the board pay cuts, and many other methods be more successful than just the cold hearted downsizing so common in corporate America today.

Sometimes managers keep people when they should not, because they don't want to be disliked. Many times when someone needs to be dismissed it is due to slothfulness, or they are in the wrong position. True compassion requires you to do what is best for them, even if they don't recognize or understand it at the time. God does it to us all of the time. We think we need or want something, but he knows we need to experience difficulties instead.

When I was a young CPA for a public accounting firm I was beginning to realize I did not like the day-to-day grind of that profession. I was getting sloppier on the details, and I no longer had much drive or passion for that type of work. I was looking for a way out, but I didn't know how. I was too apathetic to look for something else.

Suddenly the firm lost one of their largest accounts and they had to cut expenses. The managing partner, with whom I had a good relationship, called me in and was in more pain than I was about having to let me go. I immediately felt relieved, like a big burden had been lifted. I just smiled and told him he did me a big favor. Many problem employees are looking for someone to force them to go find something they really enjoy, and in which they will excel.

If you are dismissing someone due to their slothfulness the Bible is clear that if they don't work then don't feed them. Discipline is necessary in these cases to help them realize they need to work if they are going to eat. You are to still lovingly deal with them with respect and leave them with dignity.

If you are dismissing someone due to company economic troubles then you need to be as fair as possible with severance pay, and assure them that it is not due to performance. Many people's self worth is wrapped up in their career. They will blame themselves even if they were not the cause.

Once you have determined dismissal is the only solution then consider the employee's feelings more than your own. This may be a very traumatic issue for them, and they need to be treated with respect and dignity. Look for the right time and place. They will be embarrassed and sometimes angry.

Have a gentle but firm discussion, recognizing that each person handles emotions differently. Try to pick a time that will allow them to pack their belongings quietly. Recognize that there will need to be a way for them to say good-bye to others with whom they work. Consider the effect of any holidays or events in their life, which may cause it to be a bad time for dismissal.

Most of all put yourself in their place. Think about their family, their unique issues with which they will have to deal, and make it as easy as possible for them. Consider risks to the security of the business and to other employees to assure everyone will be safe if this person overreacts. Try to appropriately give them all of the details about money due them, future references, and any issues that will be of concern to them such as their family's livelihood, and their future employment possibilities.

Dismissal is very difficult for managers as well so prepare yourself mentally and emotionally. Bathe the whole situation in prayer, and let the Lord lead you through the process. Consider all sides of the issue, the business, the other employees, and the employee being dismissed. Most of all plan it out so that it is handled properly, professionally, and with great compassion and empathy to all parties involved.

If you recognize people as being your greatest asset, you will begin to realize the importance of treating them with dignity and respect. When you know the condition of the flocks God has entrusted to you, it will reap a harvest you can never measure and enhance your journey towards integrity. Pour your life into your people, and they will exceed your wildest expectations.

Part III: Finances

Putting Your Money Where Your Faith Is

"Each man should give what he has decided in his heart to give,
not reluctantly or under compulsion, for God loves a cheerful giver."
2 Corinthians 9:7

We, as managers, are not only responsible to God for the human resources he has placed in our trust, but also the financial resources. The subject of money is one of the most frequently discussed topics in the Bible, and therefore is very important to us as stewards. Financial teacher, Larry Burkett, often says, "there are no financial problems, but rather there are spiritual problems that show up in our finances." To become the stewards God has called us to be we need to continually search our heart for those spiritual problems that are limiting God's best for our life and business.

One of the key financial areas, which will uncover spiritual problems, is in the area of giving. Personal giving levels reveal our nations meager commitment to Christ, but not near as troubling as business giving. When I examine company tax returns and financial statements I may note small contributions to the local civic organizations, but rarely do I see giving to God's work through the business. This chapter will give some food for thought and guidelines on how businesses dedicated to God's work can fulfill His call to being generous to others.

Why Should I Give?

While working my way through college I occasionally needed some financial help. Many times my grandmother generously stepped forward with some cash. Little did she

know that out of my pride of being self-sufficient I kept a journal of every gift.

After college, I saved up enough money to pay her back
in full. What I counted as a loan, she considered a gift. At first
she did not want any repayment, but after my insistence she
told me to return the favor by supporting my younger brother's college expenses.

I was not as gracious as my grandmother. I couldn't resist
using my gifts as a platform for my views and agenda to be
expressed to my brother. Many years later my grandma
informed me that my brother once asked her, "Grandma, why
didn't you give me money for college instead of asking Rick
to help me? When you give, you do it with a smile, when
Rick gave it came with a lecture.

God is like my grandmother. It's all really His money, but
He uses us to distribute the wealth to those in need. We can
choose to give to His purpose and please Him, or we can
refuse, and risk Him being less generous with us in the future.
Proverbs 19:17 teaches, "He who is kind to the poor lends to
the Lord, and he will reward him for what he has done."

Giving to my brother was out of obedience, but if I had
given with grace, and a generous spirit, it would have also
been out of love.

There are many other good reasons why you should give
to God's work. Here are three.

1. He commands it. Malachi 3:8-10 says, "Will a man rob
God? Yet you rob me. But you ask, 'How do we rob you?'" "In
tithes and offering. You are under a curse-the whole nation of
you-because you are robbing me. Bring the whole tithe into
the storehouse, that there may be food in my house. Test me
in this," says the Lord Almighty, " and see if I will not throw
open the floodgates of heaven and pour out so much blessing
that you will not have room for it."

2. He deserves it. Ecclesiastes 5:19, "Moreover, when
God gives any man wealth and possessions, and enables him
to enjoy them, to accept his lot and be happy in his work-this
is a gift from God."

3. He blesses it. Luke 6:38, "Give and it will be given to

you. A good measure, pressed down, shaken together and running over, will be poured into your lap. For with the measure you use, it will be measured to you."

As we begin to understand our obligation to God we need to understand the answers to many other questions like, "How much should we give?" This requires a look at several other issues first, like tithing.

Tithing

Tithing, like many things in life, has become more complicated due to the IRS code. A business today can operate as a sole proprietor, a partnership, a Subchapter S corporation, a C corporation, a Limited liability corporation, a 501(c)(3) or an association. Although these different entities impact the tax consequences, and which entity actually pays the tithe, they don't impact the biblical admonition to give.

Let's back up and discuss what scripture has to say about this subject. To begin with the word tithe means 'a tenth'. The first reference to tithing in scripture is when Abraham gave a tenth of all of his possessions to Melchizedek, the king of Salem. It is important to note that this was prior to any commandments from God about tithing. It is also very important to understand that Melchizedek was a mysterious high priest, who according to Hebrews was greater than Abraham in spiritual authority.

Imagine someone greater than Abraham. He was the father of all nations, the cornerstone of the so-called faith hall of famers discussed in Hebrews 11, but yet he acknowledged Melchizedek's authority by giving him a tenth of all he had. Now at that time Abraham was very wealthy, so this was no small matter.

Some people believe that Melchizedek may have actually been the angel of the Lord. At any rate the moral of the story is that even Abraham, father of all nations, was willing to humble himself enough to give a tenth of all he had to God's work. He truly recognized that God owned it all.

Subsequent to Abraham God remained consistent in his

desire for us to submit ourselves to spiritual authorities, especially with our finances. He established the Levite tribe as the tribe that was to administer the spiritual responsibilities. Since God was *their* provision he did not give the Levites an inheritance of land as he did all other tribes. He wanted them completely reliant on God and his provision. His provision was to come however from the other tribes giving a tithe, and other sacrificial offerings, to the Levites.

Today's churches, if they even have the courage to teach on giving, typically focus on giving a tithe. This seems like a lot of money, especially considering that giving studies claim church members usually give less than 2.5% of their income. How does this stack up against the faithful Israelites of ancient days?

Not as well as many might think. Depending upon how you interpret a few key passages it is easy to make a case that the Israelites were expected to give 10% not once, but twice a year. In addition, they were commanded to give another 10% every three years to provide for the local Levites, aliens, fatherless, and widows.

In total this would average out to 23% of their income each year. This does not include any guilt, sin, or sacrificial giving also prescribed by God. In fairness to our current day situation it should be noted that these giving levels also covered the social needs of the society, which currently we pay taxes to cover.

Malachi 3:8 says "Will a man rob God? Yet you rob me. But you ask, 'How do we rob you?' In tithes and offerings." All through the Old Testament God makes it clear that we are to give of our increase to His kingdom work, because it all belongs to Him. Some scholars claim that the actual traditions of the faithful Israelites revealed that giving 23% of their income was not uncommon.

I know what you may be thinking, that these are all Old Testament examples, we're operating under the New Testament now. If you are thinking that because your heart really doesn't want to turn loose of your hard earned money I recommend that you stick with the Old Testament requirements, because it was a lot more stringent than Jesus' requirements.

Jesus clearly wanted us to realize that everything is God's, not just 10%, or even 23%. He told one rich young ruler to sell *all* of his possessions and give to the poor in order to enter the kingdom of heaven. He also chastised the Pharisees in Luke 11:42 "Woe to you Pharisees! For you pay tithe of mint and rue and every kind of garden herb, and yet disregard justice and the love of God; but these are the things you should have done without neglecting the others."

Considering that Jesus was a Jew steeped in the law, and the Apostle Paul was also considered a consummate Jew it is very revealing that you will not find references to tithing in the New Testament, except for the one mentioned above by Jesus. The focus instead throughout the New Testament is on giving generously, and recognizing that it all belongs to God. Paul, on many occasions emphasizes generosity and cheerful giving, rather than the dogma of the Old Testament teaching on tithing.

I've heard the New Testament position on this subject as being necessary that we hold all we have with an open hand, so that God can take what He desires. It is His already. During times of prosperity it is difficult to set aside pride of accomplishment and give credit where credit is due. We have nothing unless God favors us with His rich blessing!

According to research performed by Empty Tomb, Inc. giving since the 1950's as a percent of income has declined almost every year, to the point it is now below 2.5%. One of the more interesting statistics in their research was how high giving was during poor economic times. One of the highest percentages of income for giving was actually during the worst part of the depression in 1932 and 1933. People will rally to each other's aid when everyone is suffering.

Scripture calls us to give generously, even out of our poverty, recognizing that it is all God's. Many people believe that once they hit 10% they have completed their obligation and the rest is theirs. Since so many people have trouble giving anywhere close to 10% I like to encourage families to start moving that direction first. After they have seen how God honors and blesses that commitment then usually they begin to see that 10% is the minimum not the maximum.

There is a great book entitled "God Owns My Business" that I recommend entrepreneurs read. Mr. Tamm tells his story of how God actually called him to turn over control, and eventually all of his ownership interests, to God via a trust arrangement. The Lord richly blessed his business and his family. I have heard many stories over the years where people have said God called them to give a very significant percentage of their annual income. None of them have ever gone hungry, and all of them are excited about the blessing they receive by giving richly to God's work.

So now that we have examined giving from a biblical perspective, how do we apply it practically to business? For the business there are several issues that need to be discussed: which entity does the giving, do you give from your gross or net income, when do you give, how much do you give, and to whom?

In summary, however, the final point of this survey of Old Testament and New Testament teaching is that God is looking for us to be generous and cheerful about our giving. We need to recognize that God owns it all including our business profits and we should hold it all loosely and give when, where, and however much God directs. Now let's examine the particulars on business giving.

Which Entity Does the Giving?

Since there are so many different ways to structure a business it might be helpful for us to review briefly how these entities work. For tax purposes each entity is treated differently. A sole proprietor actually deducts their charitable contributions on their itemized deduction schedule rather than their Schedule C business form. Partnerships, Limited liability corporations, and Subchapter S corporations all receive K-1's to record the amount of charitable contributions given by the business. This information then gets deducted personally, on the itemized deduction schedule. C corporations on the other hand are more of a stand-alone entity that deducts and records its own charitable giving without it having an impact on the individual owner's tax returns.

God desires us to be good stewards with tax money as well as with all of our resources. We are to render unto Caesar what is Caesar's, but if it isn't Caesar's don't give it to him. It is perfectly legal, and I believe wise, to deduct all charitable giving that you can legally. I am sometimes asked about whether or not we should be concerned with tax consequences if we are giving from the heart.

We are to give from the heart, and not from shear tax motivations, but if you are going to give from the heart, and the IRS allows you to deduct it, you better take that opportunity. If you don't you will be squandering money on taxes that you could have given to another charitable cause. There will be times that God calls you to help specific poor or certain causes that may not be legally deductible. If you're called to give, by all means give without concern about the tax consequences.

All of this is discussed to make you aware that there are tax issues involved in business giving. If you have a choice as to whether you give from your corporation or you give personally, give from where it will be treated most favorably from a tax standpoint if all other things are equal.

Subchapter S corporations, partnerships, and Limited liability corporations allow you the flexibility to give either personally or out of the business. Either way it will flow through to your personal return.

The ownership structure of the business may be the biggest consideration in determining from which entity you give. If you have outside shareholders you will only be able to deduct the percentage of the contribution relative to your ownership interest in the business. If that is an issue you may want to make the donation directly out of your personal money.

The IRS has charitable contribution limitations on what percent of your income you are allowed to deduct. If you give too much relative to your net profit you may not be able to deduct the entire contribution. If you are a significant giver relative to your profitability I recommend you seek wise counsel from a CPA or tax attorney to assure that you maximize the dollars available for future giving.

A client of mine chose the form of his new corporation based primarily on the entity that would allow him to give the most dollars to Kingdom work. He did not want a C corporation to limit significantly how much he could give, because he had made a commitment to God to give 20% of the company profits.

Do You Give From Your Gross or Net?

A very common question about giving is, do I give from my gross or net pay? They must teach the answer to this question in seminary. Every time I have heard a pastor asked this question they always smile knowingly and give the same reply; "Which do you want blessed, your gross or net?" For anyone on a paycheck I personally believe that it is even more straightforward than that. We are to give our first fruit, which means God is first, not the IRS. Now the IRS may get their money before God, because you have no control, but in your heart God desires for you to give to him first.

Businesses oftentimes have the same question, but it is more complicated. The Bible says we are to give the first fruits of our increase. This means the increase in your material possessions. I believe this to be most closely aligned to a company balance sheet rather than necessarily the income statement. The balance sheet's primary purpose is to reflect how much of an increase you had this year in your net worth, versus previous periods. Net worth increases primarily from *net* profit.

There are businesses I have visited that believe God has called them to tithe off of their gross income. I think if you are called to do that, by all means do it. Not all businesses would be able to do that and stay in business beyond the first year.

For example, a travel agency typically only receives 8-10% of gross sales as the commission for them to cover their operating expenses and profit. If they tithed on their gross sales they would not be able to cover their rent and other expenses, and would be out of business the first month. From what I have witnessed in most businesses, any kind of giving to

God's work out of business profits would be a great improvement.

Most businesses rarely give anything from their business to God's work. They usually will make small civic donations to local organizations but it is rare to see any money donated to kingdom work. I can tell you, however, that the ones that do, have seen some great blessings.

Harry was a business owner who anxiously awaited year-end. At the end of each year, as the books were closed, he would meet with his CFO to determine how much he was going to be able to give to the Lord's work. Faithfully each year he would give at least 10% of the net profits. His small business flourished reportedly exceeding $220 million a year in revenue prior to Harry's death. The Lord so richly blessed this business that a trust was formed that has funded millions of dollars of projects.

When Do You Give?

Giving from a business is different than giving from a paycheck. When you receive a paycheck it is usually a set amount every pay period. Using the biblical concept of firstfruits with this sort of pay arrangement would mean that our tithe should come first out of our check on payday. A business, on the other hand, is much different. Some businesses reap a harvest every single day, while others may receive big checks periodically, but very infrequently, throughout the year.

In biblical times the business community was primarily farmers. The original concept of tithing related to the farmer's harvest. Since they were to give from their firstfruits it made sense that they had to wait until they had a harvest. Harvest time is seasonal depending on what crop you plant.

When a grain harvest was drawing near there would be a teaser of what was to come. There would be a small amount of harvestable crop, even though it was not yet time for the full harvest. It was from this initial harvest that the concept of firstfruits was demonstrated. The farmers would give this beginning harvest to the Lord as an offering recognizing His sovereignty and the dedication of the entire crop to God.

There are many sorts of businesses today. Some only have

a harvest once or twice a year, but many have some form of harvest each and every day. God's principle has not changed. He still desires for us to recognize His sovereignty. We should be willing to offer to Him our firstfruits. The timing is not as critical as your heart's attitude.

How often do you count your harvest? This can be a gauge as to when you should give. If you only monitor your profitability monthly, then monthly is probably a good time for giving. If it's annually, give annually. Naturally, it will need to be when you have cash to give.

Many businesses are seasonal. There may be months in which they always lose money. It's in those months when they wish to have a surplus set aside for cash shortfalls. This may be a valid reason for giving during the months with abundance, but don't hold on to the money too tightly. If God is the provider we have entrusted our life with He can make the lean months rich if we honor His commands. When you trust God solely and confidently you may find that you no longer have months that lose money.

In Leviticus 19:23-25 the Israelites were commanded not to touch the fruit of the fruit trees for the first three years, the entire crop for the fourth year was to be holy unto the Lord, so it was the fifth year before there was any harvest that was theirs. This seems like a long time to go before acknowledging the Lord with the firstfruits, but look at the requirement, they had to give the entire fourth year crop to the Lord.

If you are in the orchard business you can relate to this commandment. It takes a long time for your trees to bear fruit. Pray and ask the Lord about the timing of when you are planting and when you are harvesting. Give your firstfruits unto the Lord, regularly and consistently. Some businesses would actually have to borrow money to give during their planting season. I find no scriptural basis for borrowing to give, although I don't rule out there may come a time when the Lord calls you to do that.

How Much Do You Give?

This discussion on giving has revolved around the concept of the tithe to a great extent, so it may seem redundant to discuss how much, but it really isn't. As previously stated, the New Testament reflects more the attitude that everything is the Lord's, and the tithe is really just a starting point. For most businesses, just making the commitment to tithe from their business profits will be a big first step.

If you fear giving up that money because you feel you will need it for operating capital during your slow seasonal times, or you have some major capital expenditures coming up, stop and meditate on Malachi 3. Remember, we should really fear the Lord much more than fearing our lack of knowledge about the future.

If you do not give up the tithe, God says you are robbing him. I would rather give him the tithe, which is rightfully His, than suffer His curse, or His withheld blessing because of my fear of the future. I do not know the future, but God does. If He desires us to give, we can rest assured that if we obey that command, He can and will take care of our needs. It may not come in the way we understand or desire. We may not have the money for those capital expenditures we really thought were needed, but God's plan is sovereign. He will lead us down the right path if we are obedient to His commands.

Once you have gotten over the tithe hump, I believe the Lord will have your heart prepared to begin doing more exciting work through you. In God's eyes, if your motives are pure, you will be a better steward, and more likely to be prepared to handle further blessings and challenges.

Jesus told the rich young ruler to sell all of his possessions and give to the poor. This ruler claimed to have been faithful on all other counts. He was obedient to all the commandments Jesus asked him about. Jesus knew his heart, however, and this ruler was hanging on to his own idol, his riches. He went away saddened he couldn't, or wouldn't, measure up to Jesus' expectations.

A friend of mine took this story very literally and gave away all that he owned, approximately $5 million, and went to serve the poor. When these stories are discussed people are quick to say, "Jesus didn't mean for everyone to give all they have away" or "Jesus was using hyperbole to make a point."

Jesus' point seems clear to me. If you have an idol in your

life, even if it's all of your money, you have to give it up to serve God. If you hold open your hand and are willing to give it all to God, then you are useable for God's kingdom work.

If you are tithing from your business surplus, and think you have arrived, stop and ask God to search your heart for any idols. Ask Him to lead you to what level of giving He desires. If you still have a surplus, over your needs and any desires that God has honored, then I am sure somewhere in the kingdom there is someone with a need waiting on your plenty. God may even ask you to donate your entire business to kingdom work, like he did Mr. Tamm in "God Owns My Business."

To Whom Do We Give?

The Lord in the book of Leviticus clearly designates the Levites as the tribe that was to receive the tithes of their brothers on God's behalf. God actually gifted His tithes to the Levites so they would remember that their inheritance was from God. They were not to share in the division of lands between the tribes. Out of these tithes the Lord gave the Levites the responsibility for not only feeding their families, but to also take care of the repairs and upkeep of the temple and/or places of worship.

Now that Jesus is our high priest we don't follow the ancestral order of Levites any longer, as being God's recipients of the tithe. Rather we are to follow the principle established of providing for the faithful work of the families of God's full time servants, and the necessary upkeep of today's places of worship.

Many of today's ministries recommend that you support your local church with your tithe, and give to their ministries only after your first obligation has been met. Although I think this is a good approach, I believe scripture reflects many occasions in Paul's ministry that churches or individuals gave to further Paul's missionary activities, even though he was not necessarily the head of their local church.

Our culture today has made ministry complex. During the

first century the church was the vehicle for all ministries. There was not a need to break out separate para-church organizations, because the church worked in unity to accomplish all of these purposes. In America today we are an independent nation with complex organizational law and tax codes. Due to government social programs the church has abandoned many of the duties God has called us to perform as Christians. Many people have established separate organizations to fill these unmet needs. This leaves many choices and valid ministries that need funding.

For a business, I think there should be prayer about what kinds of ministries you desire to support, and where your tithe can be used effectively. We should be good stewards with our tithe, assuring ourselves that whomever we give it to uses it for kingdom work in an efficient and effective manner. There are a number of para-church ministries that are doing great kingdom work in which a business may like to support. Others spend more money on fundraising than they do on performing God's work.

If you review the possibilities of where you can invest your tithe be sure and consider your local church, especially if there are unmet needs. Some businesses have a specific mission or purpose for their giving. They may want to fund only evangelism activities, or activities that help minister to businesspeople, etc. I believe that these are all viable options. Personally, I use wages I draw from the business to fund my local church, but with profits from the business I try to fund ministries that help further my calling in ministering to business leaders.

God always examines the heart. If we prayerfully consider where God desires us to invest our giving, and we approach it with an open heart and generously then He will honor that commitment.

Giving Back to the Community

Many businesses recognize the need for them to give back to the community in which they operate their business, even though they usually forget to give anything to God's work.

Scripture is clear, we are to first give to the needs of our brothers and sisters in Christ, but then we are also to give to the needs of the poor, widows, and others around us. Many businesses do a poor job of managing their financial resources in this area. There are so many civic groups trying to tap into the business community's dollars that it is difficult to pick which are good investments.

In the book of Ruth we see Boaz as a model. He complied with God's commands to the Israelites to leave the excess grain from the edges of the fields for the poor in the community. The poor would come onto the land and pick up this excess, which enabled them to share in the harvest of the generous landowner. Businesses today should view this as an example.

People from civic organizations regularly approach businesses for small contributions, often times enticing them with their business being recognized in a program, etc. Not wanting to offend many in the community they agree to $50 here or $100 there without really researching the best choices for these dollars. This is a very reactive approach that is not very effective.

A simple mechanism to help businesses with this issue is to set a budgeted amount for the year. After the budget is set review the organizations you have been asked to give to in the past and consider other opportunities in your community you feel have been effective and worthwhile. Go through and prioritize this list considering their impact on the community, and considering to whom you think God has called you to minister.

It's fine to donate money and time to the local boys baseball team if you really feel it has a positive impact on the kids or the community, but it may not be fine for you to donate God's money to Planned Parenthood if you have religious convictions against this organization.

Prayerfully consider the impact of the organization, it's belief system, and what it promotes to the community. Research its history in regards to how faithful they have been in being good stewards with the resources they have been given. Do remember that every dollar spent in this area may have been more effectively used in helping in kingdom work.

Keys to Financial Success

"His master replied, 'Well done, good and faithful servant! You have been faithful with a few things; I will put you in charge of many things. Come and share your master's happiness!'" Matthew 25:21

Ongoing prosperity in business demands good financial stewardship. Managing a business can be complex. There are so many problems to solve it can be difficult to determine which issues need to be addressed first. Due to this, many businesses focus on the wrong things, or become too singularly focused. The Bible teaches that we are to know the condition of our flocks.

To assist businesses in knowing the condition of their organizations we provide clients of *Integrity Resource Center* financial report cards that give them grades in eight key financial factors. This enables them to see at a glance their strengths and weaknesses. The eight factors you will find woven into this chapter are:

1. Sales Growth
2. Gross Profit Margin
3. Operating Expense Margin
4. Return on Equity
5. Leverage (Total Liabilities/Net Worth)
6. Accounts Receivable Turnover
7. Inventory Turnover
8. Accounts Payable Turnover

Before we dive into these eight factors, let's start with the basics by listening in on a familiar mock conversation I had with Jim, a manufacturer of store fixtures. For those of you financially advanced please bear with and forgive the basic nature of some of this material. For many business leaders, this information is a critical foundation for the financial well being of their future.

"Jim, it's great to see you again. How long has it been?" I asked after settling in to the comfortable leather chair in Jim's office.

"It's been a couple of years. You probably remember quite a bit about our business from the last time you were here Rick. Let me bring you up to date on what's happened since then."

"The year after you were here last we had one of our best years ever. Sales moved up, expenses dropped, and things were more fun. Last year, however, began a different story. Our largest customer cut back their purchases over 25 percent, and we can't seem to get a handle on our expenses. Cash flow is critical, we've already lost $600,000 last year to date, and we're only two months into the new year. We need some help."

"Jim, do you have your most recent financial statements?"

"Here is a copy of our most recent income statement. Cash flow is even worse than the bottom line on that statement. I've never understood how the net profit can seem so different from what is really happening with my cash." Jim replied, with a hint of frustration, as he handed me the statement.

Income Statement

"You are not alone, Jim. One of the most common misunderstandings about an income statement is its relationship to cash flow. Many people think that the income statement is summarizing cash inflows and outflows. This is not true. The income statement (sometimes known as profit or loss statement) reflects the income and expenses for a period of time, and not necessarily cash in and cash out. It is very possible to have a profit on your income statement, but be overdrawn in your bank account. Likewise, you can have lots of money in your account, but show losses on your income statement."

"Jim, is this statement on a cash basis or an accrual basis?"

With a puzzled look Jim asked, "Can you remind me what the difference is between the two?"

"I'd be happy to. Cash basis statements are used predominately for income tax purposes. If you can be taxed on a cash basis, your taxes will usually be less than if you have to report your income on an accrual basis. The main difference between a cash basis statement and an accrual basis statement is that in a cash basis statement you do not record your accounts receivable, inventory, or accounts payable."

"The accounting profession long ago realized that to properly determine your profitability it is important to match your income with your expenses in the same time period. This is considered accrual accounting. Let me show you an example of how different accrual can be from cash."

I pulled out my pen from my planner and a yellow tablet of paper and began drawing a chart similar to the following:

	Year 2000 Cash	Year 2001 Cash	Year 2000 Accrual	Year 2001 Accrual
Sales	0	10000	10000	0
Expenses	5000	0	5000	0
Net profit	-5000	10000	5000	0

I went on to explain to Jim a year-end transaction that would dramatically alter the income statement, depending on which accounting method was used. Let's say you make a $10,000 sale of fixtures on December 15, 2000, but you give the client thirty days to pay. You will not receive the money until the next calendar year, 2001, because your year-end is December 31. Assume the product cost you $5,000 and was paid for immediately in 2000.

On a *cash basis* you would record a $10,000 sale *next* year while recording the expense *this* year. This makes it appear that you have lost $5,000 this year and made a $10,000 profit next year. This distorts what really happened and is great for taxes, but confusing from a financial management standpoint.

Jim stopped me at this point. "If I understand correctly, under cash basis I would not pay any taxes this year because I showed a loss, but I would have a tax bill next year."

"That's correct. It's great for saving money until later to pay taxes, but not if you're trying to convince your bank that you are a good credit risk."

"They probably won't be thrilled, unless they understand the full picture," Jim retorted with a new perspective.

"Now you've got it," I said as I leaned forward in my chair. "That's why accountants developed an accrual based statement. On an *accrual basis* the same transaction looks completely different. Your income statement for *this* year would reflect the $10,000 income, offset by the $5,000 expense, for a $5,000 profit."

"That's closer to reality," said Jim.

"Yes it is," I explained. "In addition you would also reflect $10,000 in accounts receivable on your balance sheet. This is a more accurate reflection of your profitability and your financial condition."

I went on to describe how valuable accrual-based statements can be in managing a business.

Jim suspiciously asked, "Is it legal to have two sets of books?"

"Yes, it is Jim. The cash basis statements, when allowable, are for the purpose of reporting the information to the IRS in a manner they allow and require. The accrual-based statement, however, is more meaningful from a financial management point of view. Therefore it is more for internal purposes, and for your suppliers, creditors, etc., unless the IRS requires you to report taxes on an accrual basis."

"Let me caution you though," I indicated, "Not everyone is allowed to use a cash basis method. The IRS recognizes which method collects the most tax so they try to discourage its use when possible. For example, in your business you carry a great deal of inventory so it is rare that a business with inventory is allowed to report their taxes on a cash basis. It is more predominately used in service industries."

As Jim digested all of this new information he stated, "I'm sorry I had you back track so much to explain all of this to me. It appears, with the information you just shared, our statements are on an accrual basis."

Jim is like many entrepreneurs. Typically when they receive tax returns or financial statements from their accountant they either file them away, or they look at sales and net profit and ignore the rest.

Jim and I broke for lunch where we met up with Wayne, the president of Jim's company, at the local diner. After we caught Wayne up on our conversation Jim queried, "Rick, you were discussing cash-basis versus accrual. Where were you headed with that discussion?"

"Once we have an accurate accrual-based income statement we can begin to compare it to previous statements. See that apple pie over there in the display case? Let's say the total pie represents your sales. It's one hundred percent of the pie. If you take a piece of pie for rent, let's say 10 percent, then you have taken 10 percent of your sales. By recognizing your gross sales as 100 percent, and each expense item as a percent of your sales, you can compare this year to last year, or to industry data."

"Imagine your telephone expense for last year was $10,000 and for this year is $20,000. Would you be alarmed?" I asked Jim and Wayne.

"It depends on how much I'm making," replied Jim.

"Good answer, Jim. You've doubled your telephone expense in one year, but what if this year sales were $2,000,000 compared to last year's $1,000,000. Would you be as concerned about the telephone expense now?"

"Probably not," said Jim.

I proceeded, "It's important to gauge your expenses relative to the volume of revenue produced. By comparing each expense item to its previous year, as a percentage of sales, you can identify the trends that may save you a great deal of money. Many times businesses allow their expenses to creep up and rationalize it away. If you compare it to the revenue being generated then you are comparing apples to apples. It's harder to justify increased expenses when you are comparing to your own previous history rather than to industry information."

Over the course of the morning it became evident that Jim and Wayne had a reasonable understanding of their income and expenses, but I knew that their problems would be found on their balance sheet.

Balance Sheet

While many people have a basic understanding of an income statement, few business people understand the purpose of a balance sheet. The income statement is for a period of time; the balance sheet is a snapshot in time. It is one specific day's financial condition. It reflects what the business owns, whom they owe, and how much is left, or in accounting terms: assets, liabilities, and net worth.

To stay in business the income statement needs to be managed well over the long term, while the balance sheet needs attention in the *short* term. If a business has accounts receivable, accounts payable, or inventory, it typically has more at risk in dollars on the balance sheet than on the income statement. If your cash is tied up in inventory and accounts receivable and it does not turnover quickly enough, you can go broke. Out of the eight key financial factors we recommend our clients to track, four are balance sheet items. These need to be monitored regularly to maintain a positive cash flow.

The net profit on an income statement helps you keep score on income versus expenses, while the net worth on the balance sheet helps you determine if the value of your business is increasing or decreasing.

After lunch Wayne, Jim, and I took a tour of their plant.

"Rick, you mentioned earlier eight keys to financial success, but I didn't get to find out more. Could you explain?" Jim asked.

"Actually I was thinking it would be helpful if we used your financial statements to examine these eight factors this afternoon. Do you have your last two year end balance sheets and income statements available?"

Wayne indicated that he had this information in his office. We stopped off at Wayne's office as he retrieved the requested information.

"Do you mind if I take a moment here to calculate a few ratios before we discuss the eight keys?" I asked as I sat down at Wayne's conference table.

"No, go right ahead, Rick, while I get Jim and me a cup of coffee."

After calculating the ratios I developed a chart for our discussion that summarized the following:

Ratios	1998	1999
Sales Growth		11.5%
Gross Profit Margin	28%	26.5%
Operating Expense Margin	25.5%	28.5%
Return on Equity	24%	-31.5%
Debt/Net Worth	1.67	1.87
Accounts Receivable Turnover	62	70
Inventory Turnover	139	187
Accounts Payable Turnover	65	96

1. Sales

"Thank you, Jim and Wayne, for giving me a few minutes to pull this information together. As I discussed earlier there are eight key factors that reveal the basic trends in almost any business. Let's begin with the area that usually gets *too* much attention."

"All profitable business organizations pay expenses with sales. The significance of sales requires monitoring. Reviewing sales growth from year to year will give an overview of the direction you are heading, especially if you break sales down by product line. I find in my consulting engagements that many businesses focus on cutting expense without identifying ways to enhance revenue. Price * quantity = revenue, and either factor or both factors can be modified to improve your gross income."

"I asked a client recently when his company had last implemented a price increase," I continued as Wayne took notes and Jim listened intently. "About ten years ago was the response. They are a union shop, and wages had increased every year for the last ten years. They had been so concerned about retaining customers, they never seriously considered a price increase, even though they were the market share leaders. Their competitors suffered for years waiting for them to increase prices."

"Information about your customers, including demographic data and likes and dislikes, are easily tracked and invaluable in planning for your future. Past sales growth is also helpful in plotting what your next year's growth will be. It will allow you the ability to determine how much capital you may need to fund that growth. Since sales drives most businesses, gain as much insight as possible from the information you have available."

Jim interrupted, "The lack of enough sales is our problem. If we could just get to $30 million I'm sure we would be extremely profitable."

"I'm glad you brought that up, Jim," I said, "A common belief by many is that more sales will cure all that ails them. Let's examine your past to see if that is true." "According to information in my file, you made over $1,000,000 five years ago on only $18 million in sales. That appears to be your best year. Sales have grown tremendously since that time topping out last year at $28 million. What was your bottom line last year?" I asked, already knowing the answer.

"Roughly a $700,000 loss," replied Wayne.

"That information would indicate to me that sales is not the problem," I concluded.

"Our sales are so volatile it is hard to manage our costs relative to sales volume," Jim complained. "One customer accounts for 20 percent or more of our total. When they pull back, we can't react quick enough."

"That is a problem that certainly needs to be solved," I agreed. "Volatile sales, whether it be seasonal in nature or dependent on the whims of one customer, is a problem companies have. It is a strategic issue as to how dependent you are willing to be on one customer. My point is, in your case sales is not really the problem."

"Going back to the first key to success, Rick, do you have a formula that you use that we can monitor periodically?" Jim asked.

"Yes, Sales Growth = (This Year Sales-Last Year Sales)/Last Year Sales"

As Jim jotted down this formula he asked, "Can we spend time at another meeting discussing solutions to our volatile sales problem, so that we can continue with learning today about these eight factors?"

I smiled, "Yes, Jim, I would also prefer that you are clear on the fundamentals before we move into the details. Before we go on, I do want to remind you that last year your sales still grew 11.5 percent, in spite of your largest customer's decreased purchases. This is another reason I'm confident sales is not the problem. Let's go next to the second key factor to achieve financial success," I stated as I steered the discussion away from the topic, which I knew would need more attention later. Jim, being the consummate salesman, had displayed previously a propensity towards believing that sales was the answer to all problems.

2. Gross Profit Margin

"If you have inventory in your business, or direct costs easily defined as cost of goods sold, then you should be concerned with your gross profit margin. The formula for this important ratio is:

Gross Profit Margin = (Sales - Cost of Goods Sold)/Sales."

"How successful you are at pricing and managing your direct costs is revealed by this ratio. Comparing the gross profit margin to industry ratios, and to your own previous periods, helps assess your effectiveness. Many people get into business unaware of what markup is typical in their industry."

Wayne stopped me, "Are you talking about gross profit or net profit?"

"Gross profit. Many people get the two confused."

Jim asked, "What kind of things should go into the cost of goods sold section of your formula?"

"Cost of goods sold includes any direct costs to manufacture or produce the product or service. This includes labor, material cost, freight, and in a manufacturing business like yours it also includes direct costs allocated to the manufacturing process such as plant rent, utilities, etc.," I explained. "Items like office rent, utilities, and other administrative expenses are reported under operating expenses rather than cost of goods sold."

"You can improve your margins by price to the customer, better supplier prices, or better inventory management. Set yourself goals for each. If you do not have a marketing niche, your gross profit margin will reflect that fault. If your margins seem too high then you may be losing profitable customers. It is more common, however, that margins are too low."

I shared this example, "Robert and Glen were clients averaging a 27 percent gross profit margin. The industry average was closer to 38 percent. They were convinced that competition would not allow them to improve in this area. I agreed with them that, in their case, pricing was competitor driven, without much opportunity for price increases. Their product costs, however, were another matter."

"Their suppliers provide perishable products so prices are negotiated daily. They had been overpaying the suppliers for product. With that knowledge, in less than three months, they had their gross profit margin up to 37 percent."

"You can test your accounting records' accuracy by comparing your gross profit margin to the markup that you apply to your product or services. If there is a significant difference, either you have a problem in your accounting system, or in the way that you have been calculating the markup."

Jim asked, "Wayne, do you feel we have been doing an adequate job of tracking our gross profit margins?"

"We could do better, but we do monitor it, and you do receive a report every month with that information," Wayne replied.

"How did we do according to your chart, Rick?" Jim asked, looking for something more tangible than Wayne's answer.

"In 1998, Jim, you had a 28 percent margin, but in 1999 it declined to 26.5 percent," I responded showing Jim and Wayne the numbers on my chart.

"That's not good," Wayne noted, "but 1.5 percent doesn't sound like much, what impact did it have in dollars?"

"1.5 percent of $28 million is $420,000."

"$420,000!" Jim snapped. "It sounds like it's critical to stay on top of the trends in this area."

Jim and Wayne both finished writing notes when Jim asked me to continue with Wayne. He excused himself to return an important phone call. Wayne and I decided to go visit the break room as I explained the third factor to financial success, operating expense margin.

3. Operating Expense Margin

As we walked I explained to Wayne that operating expense, sometimes called overhead, is the easiest area to spin out of control. "Operating expenses," I explained, "include mostly fixed expenses like rent, utilities, telephone, administrative payroll, etc. There are many opportunities to spend money in our business affairs. It is easy to spend money ineffectively. Monitoring the operating expense margin is helpful to stay on top of changes in this area."

"What's the formula?" Wayne asked.

"Operating Expense Margin = Total Operating Expense/Sales."

"The resulting percentage is useful in comparing to industry standards, previous years, and to your gross profit margin," I responded. "If you are examining profitability, comparing your gross profit margin to your operating expense margin will tell if you will be able to make a profit on increased sales."

"For example, if your business has been achieving a 27 percent gross profit margin but your operating expense margin is 29 percent, you are likely to continue losing money even if you grow sales. You will lose money faster, unless you cut overhead."

"This operating expense ratio seems generic, lumping all the expenses together," Wayne countered as we drank our soda.

"Wayne, you're right, but it does highlight the big picture of how well you are managing overhead overall. If you determine it is getting out of line, more time needs to be spent monitoring the individual expenses as a percentage of sales."

"Fast growing businesses often will increase their overhead with the anticipation of future growth," I continued. "Although sometimes this is necessary, it can be a problem if your growth is seasonal or due to positive economic factors that may change later. Once you add overhead it is very difficult to cut later, especially staff. Managing this formula on an ongoing basis can help you adjust spending prior to it getting out of hand."

4. Profitability

Jim joined us in the break room as we moved to the next category. "What are you discussing now?"

"We just finished discussing overhead," I responded. "Now let's talk about profitability. All business owners know they must make a profit to remain in existence, but how much is enough? Owning a business is an investment, although many people treat it as only a job. Knowing how well your investment is doing is necessary to compare it to other investment alternatives. This requires a consistent standard of comparison. The best comparison is return on equity."

"Is that similar to return on investment?" asked Wayne.

"Yes. Return on equity relates to a company's net worth while return on investment can be used on an individual investment in property or other assets. *Return on Equity = Net profit after Taxes/ Net Worth.*"

"Net worth is the *remaining* investment in the business; net profit after taxes is the return *on* that investment. This ratio allows you to compare the return on your business to other investments. Jim, what would you hope to receive in a return on a good mutual fund these days?" I queried.

"Maybe, 15 percent."

"A privately held business has a higher risk than a typical mutual fund," I said, stating the obvious to these long time business executives, "so you should expect your return to be higher. It is important to look over the long-term results of your investment rather than being focused solely on the short term."

"Owners' compensation is a factor often overlooked. Business owners deserve two types of returns, a return on their investment and a return for their labor."

"Pretend you earn $40,000 a year at a full time job," I explained further. "You decide to buy an existing ice cream store. $100,000 is the asking price. The current owner has been spending 60-70 hours a week managing this store, with his average net income *before* owner's compensation at $40,000."

"Is this a good deal? Someone trying to escape a job to be his or her own boss may say yes. Instead of working 40-45 hours a week for $40,000 a year, he is now going to work 60-70 hours a week for $40,000 a year and have to risk $100,000. Many people will jump on these types of situations, hoping they can do better than the previous owner. They forget the purchase price is supposed to compensate the previous owner for his previous work, not for what *you might* create in the future."

"So how do you compensate for this in your formula?" asked Wayne.

"Try substituting a reasonable salary you would pay someone to run your business in place of the current officer's salary. The resulting net profit, after this salary, can be used to divide by your net worth. This should be a closer reflection as to what kind of return you are receiving on your business investment."

"I'm afraid to ask how we've done in this category," sighed Jim.

"Actually, Jim, in 1998 you had a very respectable 24 percent return, which is a good investment, but with the losses in 1999, this went dramatically negative using up the previous gain. Your officer salaries appear to me to be within a reasonable range of necessary management compensation, so I wouldn't make any additional adjustments."

5. Leverage

"Let's move on to the fifth key to financial success, leverage. One of the most crucial ratios to a lender is the leverage ratio. You've heard about using other people's money in these get rich quick seminars, as a good thing. The banks recognize the flaw in this approach."

"The term leverage refers to the same concept as in physics of using a lever, to get more with less; like using a lever and a rock to move a large object. Many people have forgotten, however, what happens when the stick you use gets too long. It breaks. Likewise when you use too much debt in a business it goes broke."

"Leverage = Total Liabilities/ Net Worth"

"This ratio allows the lenders and you to see what level of risk there is in your business at any given point in time. By comparing the debt in your business to the amount of capital still remaining, they are able to determine how much the business owner has at risk compared to how much the lenders have at risk. The less risk they have the better."

"Many people view a bank as the place to go to have them assume your business risks. This is not the case. Banks are in the business to assist with calculated risks. Sheer speculation is left up to the owner."

"The Bible stresses you can't serve two masters, money and God. One of the evidences of this is debt. If you have more debt than equity, or you have more debt than you can pay by liquidating assets, then you are at the mercy of your creditors. This can become bondage. When you are in bondage, it is impossible to serve only God."

"In your formula, Rick, is there a number when the business is in bondage?" asked Jim.

"Jim, I hesitate to answer that because I believe this is one of those areas where God needs to lead you individually. Prayerfully consider what level of debt becomes bondage for you. Anytime you have more debt than net worth your creditors have more risk than you do and usually more control. Monitoring your leverage, setting yourself goals in this area, and getting free from bondage should be your first objectives in managing your leverage."

Wayne, while glancing at my chart noted, "According to our numbers here it appears we were at 1.67 in 1998 and now we are at 1.87. Explain those numbers please, Rick."

"In 1998 you owed 1.67 times more debt than you had in equity. Even with significant losses in 1999, this only increased to 1.87 because of the sizable net worth you have accumulated over the years. Had you not had that cushion the leverage ratio could have jumped dramatically. The good news is that even with all of your problems you have a lot more assets than debts, but the level of debt has become uncomfortable and is possibly approaching bondage for Jim."

"Yes it is," replied Jim quietly.

6. Accounts Receivable Turnover
"Have you noticed that we have transitioned from talking

about traditional income statement analysis to balance sheet factors?" I asked Jim and Wayne.

"You mean leverage versus profitability?" questioned Jim.

"Yes, leverage deals with net worth and debt, both of which are balance sheet items. The next factor is a balance sheet and income statement ratio, accounts receivable turnover. A business can be very profitable and still experience serious cash flow problems due to their accounts receivable. Let me give you an example."

"Bobby and Glen started a business in an industry unfamiliar to them. They hired sales people from the competition and put them on a very healthy commission. Almost immediately they had incredible paper profits. Months later, after the sales people had been paid their commissions and had left the business, they found that all of their sales were to the industry rejects. The company charged off over $200,000 in bad receivables. Several mistakes were made in this example, but one mistake they will never forget is that paper profits are meaningless unless you can collect the money."

"There are two primary ways to calculate your accounts receivable turnover. Many people prefer to know how many times a year their accounts turn. This is calculated: *Accounts Receivable Turnover (number) = Annual Sales/Accounts Receivable.* The other method is calculated in days. *Accounts Receivable Turnover (days) = Accounts Receivable/ Annual Sales * 365.*"

"Both of these formulas use an annual sales number and the total accounts receivable balance outstanding as of the date you are examining. If you are working with a monthly sales number you will need to annualize that number by multiplying it by twelve months."

"Which method do you prefer Rick?" asked Wayne.

"Many industries use the first method, which is fine if you know your industry averages. My preferred method however is calculated in the number of days. The reason I prefer this number for managers is that they already have a built in benchmark. What are your billing terms to customers, Wayne?"

"Net 30 days."

"If your billing terms are net 30 days, then the hope is that your customers are paying you within 30 days. If we look at 1998, you had 62 days worth of sales outstanding in accounts receivable at year-end. This is more than double what your customers have agreed to. Look at 1999-it rose to 70 days. That additional eight days of sales tied up in accounts receivable could help your cash flow significantly, not to mention what 40 days of cash would do."

"Monitoring either formula on a monthly basis will warn you if you are headed in the wrong direction. Seventy days versus your net 30-day terms is a dramatic deviation. You may have loosened your credit standards, changes may have happened in the economy or industry, or a large customer may be going bad. Regardless of the circumstances, you need to find the problem and address it immediately."

7. Inventory Turnover

"Does one of these factors deal with inventory?" Jim asked.

"Yes, Jim," I responded. "The next key to success is inventory turnover. A balance must be drawn between having enough inventory to serve your customers, and minimal levels to maximize cash."

"To determine the proper balance, you should first examine the vision you have for the company and your marketing strategy. Many businesses get caught in the trap of trying to be all things to all people. They start growing inventory because one person asked for something they didn't have."

"If your marketing strategy has a defined purpose then recognize you are not going to be able to serve everyone. Only stock what you need to serve that niche. Whenever possible try to find suppliers that can quickly respond with a short lead-time. Many of the major retailers have now gone to a just-in-time system. This system requires their suppliers to anticipate the retailer's needs through two-way communication and to fill those needs timely. This keeps the retailers carrying costs down and frees up a significant amount of cash."

Wayne asked Jim, "Should we rethink our marketing strategy, Jim? Our Swiss knife advertisements tell the customers that we can do it all. Is that what we want?"

"Just last week in our meetings with the new advertising agency they asked the same question. Let's discuss that in depth at our next sales and marketing meeting," said Jim. "So, Rick, what's the ratio to review for inventory?"

"The inventory turnover ratio is a way to determine how well you are managing your inventory."

"*Inventory Turnover (days) = Inventory/ Annual Cost of Goods Sold * 365.*"

"This formula will disclose how many days of inventory you have on hand. The inventory number is the total from either your most recent balance sheet or your actual inventory. The cost of goods sold needs to be an annualized number."

"The best way to manage inventory turns is to be familiar with industry averages, and how your marketing niche may cause your turnover to be different than the industry. Once you have this determined, set yourself a goal as to how many days worth of inventory is optimum for your business. Inventory can also be monitored by number of turns for the year rather than the number of days outstanding. The formula for number of turns is *Inventory Turns = Cost of Goods Sold/Inventory.*"

"The key is to be consistent in how you value inventory. Periodically review it in detail to assure those obsolete and slow moving goods are discounted and moved out. Freeing up cash to buy more productive goods is often better than prolonging the write-down."

"Inventory turnover sounds helpful for the big picture, Rick, but what about narrowing in on whether the problem is in raw materials, work in process, or finished goods?" asked Wayne.

"These ratios help you discover problem areas. When you determine something is out of balance, then more research is necessary," I responded. "Calculate the turnover for each component, such as raw materials, by using the same formula only substituting the individual item for the total inventory number."

"Out of all the issues discussed today inventory turnover is where your biggest opportunity lies. The industry average is around 120 days. Last year you were at 139 days that has now grown to 187 days. Forty-eight days worth of cost of goods sold is tied up in inventory instead of cash where it belongs. Your short-term cash flow problems could be solved quickly if you can find where the inventory needs to be trimmed."

8. Accounts Payable Turnover

"Gentlemen, that brings us to our last key to financial success. Accounts payable turnover. Managing accounts payable is a balancing act. Suppliers offer a source of credit to entice you to buy their products. This credit is easily abused because it comes typically at no cost. You want to use your suppliers money to leverage your sales, but you do not want to go beyond the agreed upon terms. In God's eyes that supplier relationship is more valuable than the extra cash flow or profits you might derive by stretching out their payment," I explained.

"Proverbs 3:27-28 tells us 'Do not withhold good from those to whom it is due, when it is in your power to do it. Do not say to your neighbor, Go, and come back, and tomorrow I will give it, when you have it with you.'" This seems to be a clear directive that is applicable to trade creditors. If you have agreed to buy from them on their terms then you should abide by those terms, when it is in your power to do so. As a good steward you should be careful not to overbuy, so you do have the ability to pay on time."

"There are times when you do not have the ability to pay, even after careful planning. If an account receivable goes bad unexpectedly, or gets stretched out, it can affect your ability to pay. In those cases, it is very important to communicate openly with your supplier."

"I receive many calls from businesses in financial trouble," I continued. "They will ask for help on how to deal with their suppliers. When I ask if they have talked with their suppliers about their problem, they almost always say no. Suppliers are like you. If you have a good relationship with someone, and they call and explain their difficulties, you are likely to be understanding and give them a grace period, as long as they have a willingness to pay. You will find that most of your suppliers will work with you if you are honest and communicate your progress. If, however, you have acted deceitfully, and they no longer trust you, then you will have a harder time. If this is the case, go to them and repent of your previous sins and ask if you can start over."

"Many businesses pride themselves on dragging out suppliers, thinking that they are getting a free ride. Once suppliers realize the poor treatment they are getting it is doubtful that you will get a free ride. They will begin charging higher prices, or give poorer service, to compensate for the money they are losing on your account. These two actions usually exceed the amount of savings you are getting in dragging out payment."

"The way you pay suppliers is probably the most obvious testimony you make. If you are slow paying and profess to be a Christian, they will remember and resent Christ because of your actions. If you communicate openly and honestly and treat them as you would want to be treated, they will be impressed with your testimony."

*"Accounts Payable Turnover (days) = Accounts Payable/ Cost of Goods Sold * 365"*

"The accounts payable number used is either from your balance sheet or your payables total from an accounts payable aging report. Cost of Goods Sold is an annualized number. Calculated in number of days, this ratio allows you to compare to the terms that your typical suppliers extend. When this ratio begins getting out to ninety days or more you are risking being put on COD (cash on delivery) or cut off altogether, unless you are in a unique industry."

Summary

Jim and Wayne are similar to many business leaders. They are very knowledgeable in their areas of expertise, but they could use some help in the disciplines in which they are not as comfortable. The eight factors discussed are a helpful beginning in determining the financial success of your business. If you have your last two years financial statements (balance sheets and income statements) available, try grading yourself below on each of the eight keys to financial success.

To have a comparison for grading purposes you will need to calculate these ratios for both years. Compare to last year and also to any industry data available.

I use the following grading scale:

A = Excellent
B = Good
C = Needs some improvement
D = Needs immediate attention

Financial Report Card
Formula   **Grade**

1. Sales Growth
   (This Years Sales-Last Year Sales)/ Last Year Sales   _____

2. Gross Profit Margin
   (Sales-Cost of Goods Sold)/Sales   _____

3. Operating Expense Margin
   Total Operating Expenses/Sales   _____

4. Return on Equity
   Net Profit after Tax/ Net Worth   _____

5. Leverage
   Total Liabilities/ Net Worth   _____

6. Accounts Receivable Turnover (days)
   Accounts Receivable/ Sales *365   _____

7. Inventory Turnover (days)
   Inventory/Cost of Goods Sold   *365   _____

8. Accounts Payable Turnover (days)
   Accounts Payable/Cost of Goods Sold *365   _____

Once you understand these eight factors I challenge you to use these as part of your management information each month. Most automated accounting systems can provide these ratios each month. If not, put them in a spreadsheet. Once a month a quick glance over these eight factors compared to your previous month's figures will give you the information you need to become financially prosperous.

Eliminating Debt

"The rich rule over the poor, and the borrower is servant to the lender."
Proverbs 22:7

As I speak with business owners around the country about biblical approaches to business I find that the most controversial issue is debt. Our culture has brainwashed people to believe that debt is a God given right, and that without it the whole world of business would stop. Credit is so easy to obtain that many people have a difficult time in saying no. Many people are drowning in credit addiction.

The need for convenience begins many people's problems. If you travel you need a credit card to order tickets or to rent a car. If you buy anything from mail order houses then they expect a credit card as well. It starts innocently enough, with the desire to conveniently make purchases. It quickly can deteriorate into an addiction.

What appears to be the norm today was completely foreign to previous generations. A home mortgage for more than seven years was practically unheard of as recently as the 1930's. You couldn't find anyone that would loan you money to purchase a car over a three to four year payback, and credit cards hadn't even been invented.

How did they survive without credit? They used cash. Yes, sometimes they might have credit available to them at the local store, but it was always paid back in full when the harvest came in.

Easy credit has become a curse. In spite of the roaring economy in the 1990's bankruptcies skyrocketed, personal and business debt mushroomed, and more people are in financial bondage.

Almost every time there is a new credit product introduced in the banking industry it has been driven by people who benefit the most from higher prices. Imagine visiting a car dealer with your $10,000 budget. The first question out of the salesman's mouth is how much can you afford to spend a month.

He or she doesn't care how much you can afford to spend overall. If you tell them a monthly figure you will likely be steered to the most expensive car they can find. Then they begin discussing your financing options. A five-year loan or their latest leasing program suddenly becomes the standard. Greed, envy, or your ego may become weapons used against your desire to only spend $10,000 cash.

Credit has also had a dramatic impact on prices. The 5 year car loans, the leasing programs, the 30 year mortgages all have been driven by sales people and bankers that make more off of you with credit. Prices have risen dramatically over the years because of these looser credit policies. Reflect on your home.

Could you have afforded to purchase the home you currently live in if you could have only gotten a seven-year loan instead of a 30-year? I doubt it. This price escalation has made it more difficult to purchase major items within your budget. Inflation comes from easy credit and its related price increases. If our entire culture operated on a cash only basis there would not be much inflation. What inflation would appear would be from improvement in overall productivity.

Debt is, in its simplest of terms, a presumption on the future. You are buying something today with the anticipation that you will be able to pay it back tomorrow. Our bankruptcy statistics show that this presumptive approach doesn't always work. Matter of fact it's working less and less. Ecclesiastes 11:2 tells us "Give portions to seven, yes to eight, for you do not know what disaster may come upon the land." When you take on debt you are presuming that no disaster will come upon you.

Is Debt a Sin?

There are no commandments against debt, but there are

also no examples in scripture where debt was used positively. Debt is discussed a great deal in the book of Proverbs as well as in Luke and other places. Quotes such as "the borrower is servant to the lender" are an indication of God's warnings to us about debt.

When Jesus said man couldn't serve two masters, he must choose between God and mammon, He was showing us some insight into debt. If your debt causes you to serve your lenders how can you serve God also? A small debt to some can be huge to others. It is an individual decision to determine when you are in bondage to your lender.

Some warnings as to when you have crossed the line are as follows:

•Your debt exceeds the value of your assets. Your asset value should be determined by considering how much you would receive if you had to liquidate immediately, including all selling costs and necessary discounts.

•When you begin having anxiety about the outstanding debt.

•When your cash flow is insufficient to make the loan payments without going further into debt.

•When lenders turn you down for a loan. They are trained to only take calculated risks. If you are declined on a loan request it probably is either due to not enough collateral, not enough cash flow, or poor credit history. Any of these reasons for a decline should cause you to stop and reconsider your decision.

•When you are borrowing new money, even though you haven't repaid other outstanding loans within their agreed upon terms.

•If you were to completely lose the asset that secures the debt and still have to pay the debt, could you?

In summary, although debt may not be a sin, it is certainly a snare to many. If you are presuming upon the future to repay your debt God may surprise you. The Bible teaches, "The Lord's blessing comes without curse." If God really wanted to bless us He could easily provide cash rather than a loan.

There are people so conservative that they have crossed

the line into hoarding. They may never take any risks until they have every last dime up front, even if God has clearly instructed them to take a step of faith. Once again, it boils down to, "where is your heart?" If your heart is focused on hoarding, or lenders, or anything that replaces your trust in God, then you are outside of God's will. If you, however, are waiting patiently on God's timing, not jumping ahead and presuming on the future, then you are likely to be pleasing to God.

When to Use Debt

A businessman had an opportunity to buy an apartment complex at a significant discount from the appraised value. After thorough investigation he found it was structurally sound, had great cash flow, high occupancy, and all of the other attributes you would want in an apartment complex. He and his partner had significant cash to invest, but not enough for all of it. They decided to borrow 50% of the cost of this project, which required them to personally guarantee the loan.

Soon after they bought the project, it was discovered that there was an environmental problem. Prior to the purchase they had checked out the typical environmental problems. This turned out to be a brand new concern of the Environmental Protection Agency that was not previously recognized as an issue.

The apartment complex had to be completely leveled. No environmental insurance coverage existed, no potential for recouping their investment, and no way out of their personal obligation on the debt. One of the partners filed bankruptcy; the other supposedly took years to pay back the obligation.

This story illustrates what Solomon teaches in Ecclesiastes, when he said, "no one knows what the future might bring." Many people would excuse this example as a run of bad luck. There are no coincidences, only God knows the future. When we presume upon the future, regardless of our level of caution, we run the risk of unforeseen consequences.

Am I trying to claim that no one should ever borrow

money? No! I am saying when you do, you take a risk regardless of how careful you may be. Debt should be the last resort rather than the first. It should be carefully and prayerfully considered and you should give God ample time to provide in other ways first. Debt should be an individual decision based on your circumstances and God's leading, not solely based on the belief that it is the only way you can get your deal done.

Many people call me in the process of starting a business. Inevitably, they discuss getting a loan from the bank, usually for the entire investment needed, as if it is a foregone conclusion that you must borrow money to start a business. Rarely have they considered other options, like an investor, God potentially surprising them with a windfall, or that maybe this business isn't God's will.

God desires the best for His children. If He wants one of His children to start a business He can provide all of the funds, without a loan. But He's waiting for us to ask. Nothing significant happens without prayer. Pray and ask that the Lord provide the funds for your business. Wait patiently, with your eyes wide open, to see what God is doing. If nothing happens, (it may not look or seem like you anticipated) then you need to seriously consider if you are embarking on a journey outside of God's will.

I experienced God's provision when I started Integrity Management. At the bank where I had been working I had negotiated an employment contract with eight months of severance pay should the bank be sold. When the bank sold I discovered a loophole as big as a Mack truck in the agreement that would allow the buyer to demote me, cut my pay, and drag me out until I quit.

The local person whom I was negotiating with made several promises that he did not keep. Although he had promised to honor my contract he was having second thoughts. In the meantime, with God's direction, I had taken his original promise and had begun making commitments to start Integrity Management.

We fervently prayed for God's intervention. We were too far down the road to stop Integrity Management, but it really looked like we were not going to get any money. Then God intervened in an interesting way.

The purchaser of the bank was a closely held holding company. They did not yet know if I was staying or leaving, because I had not yet finalized my decision. The CEO did not have an employment contract and the fact I did seemed to be an issue with him. He directed the local bank president to buy out my contract because "no one in this organization has ever had an employment contract, including me, and we're not starting now."

God knew I would need eight months severance to support my partner and I while the business was in its infancy. We didn't need nine months or seven months, but eight. We made a commitment that the business would not borrow money, unless it was personal money from ourselves, and with God's blessing we maintained that pledge.

These examples are shared with you in the hopes that you rely on God rather than on debt. The answer to the question, "When do you use debt in business?" is *rarely* and *sparingly*. It is necessary to prayerfully consider God's will and timing for your circumstance.

If you are comfortable that debt will not become a master to you, either now or in the future, then maybe God will condone borrowing. If so, take it slow, get lots of good counsel, and use prudence.

This topic is sensitive to many and my approach is conservative, but I meet with business owners regularly that are filled with pain, their marriages are coming apart, and they have no idea how to climb out from underneath the mountain of debt. God had a better plan for them. As the body of Christ let's try to become lenders rather than borrowers, experiencing blessings rather than curses.

Surety

The concept of surety is mentioned in the Bible often, but is unfamiliar to many believers. Surety in the Hebrew meant to bail, or post bail for someone or something. Proverbs warns often not to become a surety for another. In today's terms this concept relates to personally guaranteeing another's debt, or to pledge assets for a debt. In business it usually relates to a person guaranteeing a loan to their business, or cosigning a note for someone else.

In biblical times I believe this concept was a little less complicated. There were no corporations to shelter individuals from liability. Corporations are usually formed to share ownership, to limit liability, and/or to reduce taxes. We are such a litigious society that corporations are formed many times to avoid a potential lawsuit from parties that believe they have been harmed in some manner by a business' activities.

If everyone operated under the principles in the book of Leviticus about justice then we would not need as many corporations. Business owners would be responsible for their actions, and parties interested in suing them would have defined lines as to what they could sue for and what they couldn't.

Instead we have developed a system, thanks to our courts creating their own ambiguous laws, that allows anyone to sue anybody for anything without penalty. If you are wealthy you can sue someone and spend enough money until you break him or her, whether or not you were right. It's because of these possibilities that many business owners began forming corporations to shelter themselves from foolish suits. Over time business owners started using the corporations to shelter themselves from legitimate claims as well.

Some Christian teachers recommend you not personally guarantee your own corporation's debts because this violates the biblical principle of surety. Although there is some merit to this I think there is another aspect to consider.

Years ago, when I owned a car rental agency, I formed a corporation primarily to shelter me from any liability of someone recklessly using one of my cars and trying to make me or my insurance pay for their wrongdoing. At the time I liquidated the business I had a few outstanding supplier bills.

These suppliers technically had contracted with the corporation without requesting or receiving my personal guarantee. This is commonly the case with suppliers and it is a risk they run. I had enough money to pay everybody that the business owed except for one supplier, our trash service. I had no personal obligation legally, so when they called I explained to them that their debt was with the corporation and it had been liquidated, and they were out of luck.

God is such a patient God that when He knows we need to learn a lesson He will wait until we are ready to listen. It took me thirteen years before I was ready to listen, but one day I decided to dedicate my quiet time to laying all of my past sins on the altar for forgiveness. I dug deep into my past and prayed that God would reveal all of my sins one by one.

Well He did. It was an expensive day. God wanted me to make restitution on several personal and financial matters. One of them was the trash service. The Lord revealed to me that it didn't matter if I had a legal obligation or not, what mattered was that I, as an individual, had made a vow to that company. If they provided the service they believed I would see to it that they would be paid.

I also realized that God doesn't care about the money. If it hurts our testimony we should pay the obligation and make it right. Remember Jesus told Peter, when the Pharisees asked him about paying taxes, that although they were of the heavenly kingdom, not Caesar's, they should pay anyway so that the Pharisees would not stumble.

I sent them a check and a letter, giving God the glory for their payment of the long overdue bill. I received a letter back from a sister in Christ in their accounting department. She claimed the letter touched several people in their office. In memorial of that gesture they contributed the money to a local church.

From my experience the principle I learned is that if we make a vow, whether it be for us personally or as a corporate officer, that vow is to be kept. If, however, you take out a loan for your corporation, and you specifically agree that you are not personally responsible for the debt then you have made it clear as to the risk they are taking and that will prevent you from becoming a surety on that loan. They will have to rely on the collateral and/or credit of the corporation and not you for repayment.

There are very few financial institutions, however, that will make any small business loan without a personal guarantee. God is awesome though and He might allow it if you are diligent to stick to His principles.

As far as cosigning a note for someone, avoid it! If they need a cosigner it is because they cannot get credit on their own. If you cosign the odds are very high you will be the one paying back the loan not them. I don't personally ever remember a cosigner escaping without having to make some payment. Avoid it like the plague.

How To Get Out of Debt

If you are like many business people you may already be in debt, so the above warnings are a little late. In 1981 I was paying close to 21% interest on an SBA loan. It's pretty hard to make any business work at that kind of interest rate. That was a painful period of time in my life. Debt in business has a way of causing pain to owners, staff, family members, suppliers, and sometimes customers. It is a heavy burden to many.

Unfortunately there are consequences for our actions that do not always resolve themselves easily. If it took you several years to get into financial trouble it won't go away overnight. There are steps, however, you can take to help you through the process.

The first step is to recognize the problem. Many entrepreneur's wives call me upset because they know their husband's business is failing, but they can't get their husband to discuss the problem, or to even to acknowledge that there is a problem. Our pride can allow us to be deceived into thinking we have a temporary problem that will soon go away. If you have a mountain of debt it usually isn't a temporary problem. It is a dilemma that needs to be tackled with much diligence and perseverance. If you are too close to the situation please seek outside help to give you a clear understanding of the problems in your business.

Many entrepreneurs are salesmen. When they have too much debt they often confuse themselves by believing their problem is sales. They ignore the debt and go out and sell more. This can help in some cases, but often times these businesses are undercapitalized causing additional cash flow problems. Now they have even more money tied up in accounts receivable without the capital to finance the growth. Many times they also are operating on margins that are actually negative so that the more they sell the more money they lose.

If you are struggling in your business, objectively examine the problems and determine the core underlying problems. There really are no financial problems, but there are spiritual problems that reveal themselves in your finances. If you can't control spending maybe you are coveting what others have in their business. If you have lots of debt maybe you didn't wait on God's perfect timing. If you prayerfully seek the Lord's counsel he will be faithful to lead you to the answers.

Once you have recognized the problems fix the spiritual problems before going further. "If you confess your sins God is faithful and just to forgive us our sins."

Many people call me about consolidating their loans in order to ease their cash flow. There can be times that this makes sense, but I recommend that you don't try this until you are confident that you have worked through the underlying spiritual problems. If you don't fix the bad habits a consolidation loan will relieve the pressure and you will have a false sense of security. Then your bad habits will continue in the form of new debt. The problem gets worse instead of better. Only consolidate after you have fixed the true problems.

Now that you have recognized the problems and have worked on fixing them it is time to roll up your sleeves to tackle the debt. The first thing to remember is there are only three ways to eliminate debt.

•Dispose of assets and use the proceeds to pay off debt.

•Improve or use cash flow effectively to reduce the debt more gradually.

•Get a capital injection, either through an outside investor or by the hand of God gracing you with a miraculous source of cash.

Let's examine the first possibility. Many businesses have unproductive assets that are either lying dormant or are not being used effectively. First, determine the minimum level of assets you need to operate your business. Next, take an inventory of what you own. Sometimes businesses have fully depreciated assets that still have value. Look for these types of opportunities to raise cash.

In many businesses the biggest opportunities are right in front of them. If you have accounts receivable and inventory in your business you might have overlooked the most likely reason for your increased debt. Many entrepreneurs focus on managing their income statement and completely ignore the balance sheet. There are usually many more dollars tied up in the balance sheet. If you do a poor job of managing your inventory and accounts receivable the amount of cash tied up can be incredible.

Let me give you an example as to how you can go about squeezing cash out of your assets. Let's assume you are a distributor of auto parts that currently has $5,000,000 in sales. You sell to retailers on 30-day terms. You began business with the philosophy of providing niche parts to retailers, allowing you higher margins.

Over time your customers liked your service so well they began asking you to carry more traditional parts. Sales have expanded nicely but so has your debt. After the pain became unbearable you decide to examine your business to determine what you can do differently.

As you began looking for ways to raise cash to reduce debt you decide to take a closer look at your inventory and accounts receivable. You look back over the last three years and find that your average customer three years ago used to pay you in 35 days, but now it has increased to 50 days before the average customer pays. You next examine your inventory and find that when you were more focused on niche parts you typically had 150 days of inventory on hand but recently you find that it now is closer to 190 days worth of inventory.

Once armed with this information you realize that there are several possibilities to improve this situation. You can tighten your credit policies by implementing a quicker follow-up on delinquent accounts and offer a 1% discount if paid within 10 days. You can go through your inventory and identify the slow moving inventory. You mark it down and move it out.

Next you make a determination of which parts you will

continue to sell, keeping a sharp eye on the original focus of niche parts. These steps after implementation have succeeded in lowering your average accounts receivable back to 35 days, which freed up over $200,000 and your inventory has decreased to 160 days, which freed up an additional $200,000. In this example, by taking these actions this business has reduced debt by over $400,000 without hurting profitability. Actually profitability was improved by the reduced interest expense, and the extra time wasted previously on handling more inventory and slower accounts.

The second method of reducing debt is the most painstaking and slow, but usually the only solution. If you remember the Proverb that says, "Steady plodding brings prosperity, but hasty speculation brings poverty" you will understand that diligence is called for in reducing debt as well.

Examine your business closely, fix the underlying problems, and begin increasing revenue, improving gross profit margins, and decreasing overhead. Once you have excess cash flow coming in again then you can begin working down the debt. It is very helpful to schedule out each loan, listing the beginning balance, the outstanding loan amount, the payment amount, the interest rate, the collateral and the maturity date of the loan.

Next, list each loan in order according to size. Once you have your list it's time to determine who to pay, when, and how much. Naturally, you need to pay the committed payment amounts first. If you can't even pay these amounts then it is time to go to your creditors with a reasonable plan as to what you can do, and timing as to when things might improve.

Many people cannot pay the entire amount of payment owed so they don't pay anything. They don't communicate with the creditor; they just bury their head in the sand hoping that it will go away. This is not an appropriate witness. Regardless of how painful it may be, and how much your pride is hurt, you need to go to them one on one and explain your situation and ask for their help. Most business owners have had similar difficulties at some point and are more than willing to help. If they think you are sincere they will usually work something out. Actually, most of them will be amazed you had the courage to communicate your troubles, rather than hiding and forcing them to chase you.

Once you have begun paying the agreed upon amounts, then any excess cash flow should go towards debt. The reason many businesses never get out of debt is that once their cash flow improves they give themselves a raise or a bonus and increase their personal lifestyle, rather than using the money to reduce debt. This increased personal lifestyle actually becomes a curse later when the business suffers an economic downturn. Any excess cash flow should be applied towards debt until you whittle away at it and it's gone.

In a business there are many variables as to which debt should be reduced first. Many people are accustomed to tackling the highest interest rate first. Although this is usually a serious factor to consider, it is not necessarily the best for you. Other factors that may influence your decision may include the collateral pledged to the lenders and their lien priorities, which loans have personal guarantees that you desire removed, and which debts would give you a sense of accomplishment.

If all debts are equal in regards to your personal obligations, and lien position priority of lenders, then normally I would recommend paying off the smallest debt first. This will eliminate a payment that can be applied to the next smallest debt and will give you an initial sense of accomplishment. Sometimes, however, one creditor has a first lien position on a piece of collateral that you need released. For instance, if you had a company truck needing to be replaced soon, and there is still a loan on it, you might need to apply your excess to that loan first in order to free up the collateral.

Diligence is the key in reducing debts. If paying off a small loan gives you a sense of accomplishment then do that first to assure that you stay on track. If your marriage is suffering because of your spouse's concern over a personal guarantee, or your home being pledged to a certain loan, then work towards getting that released. Develop a plan that works for you and stick to it.

The third way I've mentioned to reduce debt is to have a

capital infusion. Our culture is so focused on debt as the only vehicle for funding, and lenders have made it so easy to obtain credit, that other alternatives are not considered.

There are ways to obtain capital other than debt. If you have a viable venture that expects a good return you might be able to find investment capital. For most small businesses this comes in the form of family, friends and employees. There are venture capitalists available, but they will typically require you to be in a high tech or fast growing industry, with a great deal of growth potential. Their minimum may be $3 million or more.

If you find an interested party be very careful on the front end to answer all of the potential questions and issues that may come up and address them in writing. A partner in business can be worse than being indebted to a lender if not well thought out and structured properly.

A big void in the Christian marketplace is someplace to go to put Christian investors with Christian entrepreneurs needing money. I occasionally work on these deals individually but I get a number of requests from across the country from entrepreneurs seeking capital in which they won't have to be unequally yoked. Although I believe that believers should only be yoked with believers in a business relationship sometimes the conduct of Christians in business is even worse than partnering with a venture capital firm.

In working out a deal with a potential investor in your business there are several issues you need to cover. The most important issue is an exit strategy for both parties. If you believe you need the money to stay in the business for 10 years or more, and they desire to be bought out in 5 or less, you have a big problem. It is important that you sit down and have a very frank discussion up front about all of the what-ifs. What if the investor doesn't like your performance, what if you think your investor is too demanding, what if you need more capital for further growth, what if one of you dies? All of these and more are very feasible possibilities in a partnership that need to be addressed before beginning this relationship, and need to be addressed legally in writing.

Usually the first issue the investor wants to address is the question of how much return and what stake of the company will they have. This is usually where most deals fall apart. Many entrepreneurs believe that although they don't have any money, their idea should give them the right to controlling interest in the company. The investor, on the other hand, wants some assurance that if your performance isn't what you promised, that they have a way to get you out, so they usually expect control. The best way to work this out is to sit down and discuss each person's goals.

The goal isn't usually to have control of the company; it's usually to have some control over their destiny if things go wrong. Most of these issues can be addressed in another manner legally without control of the stock being the pivotal issue. Maybe control of the stock is an event of default, but not necessary to give up on the front end. If control is a big issue with the entrepreneur sometimes it can be accomplished by finding 5-7 smaller investors that are sharing more equally in the risk so that no certain one of them is seeking control.

Investors usually require a much bigger return then what you might pay a lender, but they usually are sharing the risk with you without you having to personally guarantee any indebtedness. Some investors prefer to be repaid much like a loan with a monthly payment that is fixed; others want a straight percentage of the profits that they may or may not be willing to retain in the business for future growth. Each deal is unique and needs to be structured around each person's needs.

Many people try to buy a business with owner financing. Sometimes this can work out well if it helps you avoid personal liability on the loan. Make sure that the business is the only security for the debt so that if it doesn't work out they get the business back, but you walk away without further risk. One big factor, however, is who owns the business until it's paid off, and are you going to fall into the unequally yoked trap in the interim.

Study the story of Joseph's stewardship over Pharaoh's property. Buried in that story is a very interesting approach that I think may be useable at times in structuring deals. After all of the people had run out of grain, they first sold their live-stock, next they sold their land, then they finally sold them-selves into servitude to Joseph. Joseph suddenly became the owner of all of the land of Egypt and the people in it. Now he could have been like many rulers and made the people work the land for just room and board, but he didn't.

Joseph gave them seed to plant their next crop and then told them that he wanted 20% of the harvest given to Pharaoh, but the remaining 80% was for them to use for seed and provisions for their families. From today's worldly per-spective this seems foolish because I have seen a lot of share-cropping arrangements at 50/50 or 60/40 but never 20/80. This was the first recorded sharecropping arrangement.

Look at the positives to both parties. The people rejoiced and praised him for his graciousness because this was far in excess of what they could have ever expected. But more importantly, look at what Joseph accomplished. He now assured himself that these people were going to work the land with all of their heart which would produce a much more productive crop. He also set himself up for potential buyers for the land in the future, at probably a higher value to the land because of their diligence in working the land. I think this is a true example of a win-win relationship that God worked out through Joseph.

In any partnership be very diligent to know all you can about each other, personally and professionally, so that you don't become a bad testimony to others around you. Determine how each type of decision is going to be handled. For instance 50-50 partners rarely ever work for long because it is fraught with potential failure. Who decides the ties? Consider giving swing vote stock to a party, or parties, whom you both trust for tie breaking problems. Investment capital can be a great way to stay out of debt, but it still needs to be approached very cautiously.

Summary

God desires you to serve Him, not creditors. If you desire to build a prosperous business, make a commitment to trust God rather then debt.

Still Putting God First

"I have seen another evil under the sun and it weighs heavily on men: God gives a man wealth, possessions and honor, so that he lacks nothing his heart desires, but God does not enable him to enjoy them, and a stranger enjoys them instead. This is meaningless, a grievous evil." Ecclesiastes 6:1-3

King Solomon reportedly penned the above verses in Ecclesiastes. Solomon was speaking from experience. If you remember the story, Solomon is the one who asked for wisdom when God offered to give him whatever he requested. Since God was so pleased that Solomon was concerned enough for the people in his kingdom that he asked for wisdom, God decided to also give him tremendous wealth. This great wealth later became a curse to him, as he turned to his many wives' gods and chased after meaningless pursuits.

From Solomon's writings you can tell it bothered him that someday he was going to die, and all he worked for was going to be turned over to someone else less faithful. In fact, because of Solomon's sin his son Rehoboam ultimately lost reign over the vast kingdom (ironically, because he showed a total lack of wisdom). The people split and Rehoboam wound up with a much smaller kingdom. The lesson that Solomon learned was that all wisdom and prosperity is meaningless if God isn't still first in your life.

Overcoming Pride and Greed

If you are obedient in following God's commands in your business, you will likely experience prosperity somewhere along the way. If that becomes true you will be on a dangerous journey. Jesus taught that it was easier for a camel to go through the eye of a needle, than it is for a rich man to get to heaven. Many people stop there without reading the following verses. The disciples were concerned about this statement so Jesus clarified it by telling them "all things are possible with God."

From this passage I conclude it is possible for a rich man to get to heaven, and I believe we will see many there, but we will see fewer rich than poor. This will be, to a great extent, due to pride and greed. What tremendous stumbling blocks these two sins can become.

Consider the businessperson for whom everything begins clicking. Sales are growing, they hire more staff, the product or service gets rave reviews, sometimes even national recognition, and now this person is too important or busy to spend time with their former friends or employees. Remarkably, they begin telling everyone how brilliant they are for all they have accomplished. God is never mentioned when it's time for credit to be given.

Then the newspaper and magazine articles begin. It's at this point, as a former banker, I became nervous. Dozens of times I would see a customer of the bank featured in the local newspaper. It was then I knew I better get out there right away. Inevitably, soon after the articles we would be adding this customer's loan to our bank's problem loan list. As Proverbs 16:18 says " Pride goes before destruction, and a haughty spirit before stumbling."

A previous client experienced rapid growth. They took a good idea, and a strong sales person, and grew rapidly and profitably. After their third year in business they began winning small business of the year awards, Chamber of Commerce awards, and much publicity. They were on top of the world.

The following year sales began dropping while expenses continued to escalate. By the end of the year they had lost a significant amount of money, but were still undaunted. They plowed into the next year still optimistic, but things got worse. They found that the sales person had been extremely dishonest, and their information was not accurate.

It was becoming desperate. The bankers were nervous, and things were getting worse. As I analyzed the historical data it became apparent the warning signals were in their financial statements as far back as their most profitable year.

As they were out spending time in the public eye their business was already unraveling, but they were too busy with outside activities to recognize the coming problems.

Pride and greed are common issues that seem to come with success. It has been said that a lot more people fall out of church during times of prosperity than do during times of poverty. When everything seems to be going your way it's easy to feel you were the reason for the success rather than God's blessing. The haughtiness that comes with pride makes it difficult to see our own sin and makes it near impossible for God to use us effectively in ministry.

Greed, on the other hand, allows us to make poor decisions. When God wants us to choose people we choose money. God is much more concerned about relationships, and the impact our decisions make on people, than he is money. When we allow greed to take over we choose money rather than people.

Change the amount you are discussing when you are making a choice between people's needs and money. If you were talking about a decision that may cost you $10,000, for instance, ask yourself, would you make the same choice if it were only $10. If you would, you are probably leaning the right way, but if not then you may be selling your integrity for the sake of money.

Pride is one of the most difficult attributes to see in ourselves. We truly do not want to think of ourselves as prideful, but yet most of us will struggle with this at some point in time, if not constantly. It requires periodic self-examination to flush this problem out. Take time regularly to open yourself up for God to reveal your sins. If there is pride in your life ask God to show it to you, and how to deal with it. Accountability is very useful in having someone help you to see when you are slipping into the sin of pride.

If God has blessed you with success and prosperity in your business don't let it be robbed by pride and greed. Stay on top of where you are in your relationship with God. Use the prosperity to honor God rather than dishonor him.

Hanging On to God and Prosperity

Do you still love God with all your heart, mind, and soul? Are you still as committed to the Lord as you were when your business was struggling to survive? These are a couple of the questions on which you need to ponder if you've been experiencing prosperity in your business. God wants you humbly serving him regardless of your stature in the community.

Many people believe that going to church is for the purpose of spiritually nourishing themselves personally. Certainly it is important to receive some spiritual refreshment, but we must also remember that we are part of a body of Christ. If we forsake our role in that body by dropping out of fellowship with others, then we are robbing the body of our gifts and contributions to the encouragement and development of others.

Steve Camp, a Christian musician, discussed on a radio program that many of the top Christian musicians do not have a church to which they are accountable. It would get tiresome being followed around in church, or constantly bothered, but the book of Hebrews is clear, we should not give up on the fellowship of believers, as they are to be an encouragement to us, and us to them.

The church is also the accountability structure God uses to keep His children in line. If we shun that tool of God then we will quickly find ourselves rudderless without the effective anchor God designed to hold us accountable.

If you recognize the truth that God is the provider of all prosperity, then you will also remember he can take it away as fast, if not faster, than he gave. (Study the book of Job if you have any doubts.) It is even more critical during times of prosperity that you cling to God. Go praise Him, spend time with Him, and love Him with all your heart, mind, and soul.

Give Yourself a Checkup

In the first chapter I outlined an exercise of reviewing your priorities. This is a continual exercise. It is too easy to stray far away from God, especially during times of prosperity. Periodically, schedule time alone to give yourself a checkup.

1. Review Your Checkbook

Examine how you spend your money. Is your level of giving where God has called it to be? Are you taking care of the needs of your family, your employees, and any poor and/or needy that the Lord has brought your way? Or instead, is your money now going towards toys? Maybe your new boat or new lake house has become more important than the poor or needy.

God does want to give his children good gifts, so it is not necessarily wrong to accumulate some possessions, but he is more concerned about the needs of His people. In Acts the believers all began pooling their resources so that not one of them had a need. In the culture we live in today it is so difficult to discern between needs, wants, and desires.

One day I was in the break room with several employees from where I was working when one of the ladies made a comment about something that she really *needed.* I made a casual response, "Is it something you need or something you desire?" That comment spawned a very interesting conversation. The women in that room thought my question to be a profound one, as we discussed the differences between needs, wants, and desires.

That conversation drove home to me that very few people today seldom really consider the difference between a need, a want, and a desire. Fifty years ago you would have probably been hard pressed to find anyone that believed a telephone or a television was a necessity, while today you would have a difficult time finding very many people that think these are not necessities.

As you prepare to buy items in the future ask yourself if this is truly a need, a want, or a desire. As you begin weeding out more of the desires and wants you may find that you have a whole lot more disposable income for giving to God's work and for yourself.

Establish long term goals for your wants and desires. If you set standards today as to how big a house you want, how

nice of a car you would like to have, etc. you will set a benchmark for yourself that later you may not be as inclined to
change. When you set your standard, commit any excess over
this wish list to God. If you don't do it now, when you have
enough to buy those things you will just establish an even
higher standard.

Remember the times in your life you received a raise,
what was the first thing you did? If you are like most people
you went out and committed money to new toys or a higher
standard of living. Surveys that have asked people their definition of rich have concluded that it is just a little more than
what they currently have. Don't fall into that trap. Set yourself
a wish list and allow God to use the excess.

2. Review Your Schedule

One of the most difficult things to do when business is
booming is to protect my quiet time with God. I prefer starting my morning with bible study and quiet time in prayer.
When the schedule starts getting full, because of lots of activity in the business, it is easy to try and jam everything into
your calendar. When this happens I usually begin looking for
additional time to accommodate a meeting with someone. It
oftentimes becomes a breakfast meeting, which is usually
when I would be in my quiet time. Before long instead of just
a breakfast or two I have a whole week full of them, and I find
I have missed my most important time with God.

Remember your priorities. It is easy to think in terms of a
customer's need, or the big deal you may land if you have that
breakfast meeting. If you are like me I can rationalize that
God will understand. Don't get me wrong; I don't believe we
should place guilt on ourselves if we miss a quiet time here
and there. When it becomes apparent, however, that you are
not having any quiet time, because you have placed a customer as a priority over God, then I think you will have a real
problem. God is a jealous God and he wants to be first in our
life.

If your life becomes chaotic because of your business,
maybe it's time to stop and review your schedule. How much
time have you spent with God this week? When was the last
time you were alone with God for a retreat of rejuvenation?

What does your current schedule tell you about your priorities? Have you had time for your family? Are you using your time wisely? Did you find time for the TV, but no time for God? These sorts of questions will help you to refocus your priorities.

In the front of my daily planner I have written my personal mission statement and a list of priorities in my life. As I plan my week I try to review these items and ask myself what is the most important thing I can do today to achieve my long-term objectives and fulfill my personal mission. I don't always stay on track but this process helps me to stay on track more than I would otherwise.

There is something powerful about asking yourself what I would like certain people to say as eulogies about me upon my death: people like my family, my employees, my customers, my suppliers, my friends, my board, my pastor, and most of all what is God going to say when I stand before Him. What would it take each day for you to achieve those dream eulogies? Develop a list and keep those long-range goals before you somehow each day.

A periodic checkup, especially during busy times, is very useful in reviewing your schedule and determining if your priorities are being maintained. Do not let a full month go by before you realize how off track you are with God, your family, friends, and the priorities that really matter in the end.

The Fear of God

When prosperity is all around us it's easy to become arrogant or haughty. Humility is a trait not seen as frequently in people experiencing prosperity, as it is when the Lord has taken the wind out of their sails. There was a song many years ago by Mac Davis that said "Lord, it's hard to be humble when you know you're so good." There is a lot of truth in the fact that it is hard to be humble, however, Jesus told us that none of us are good. We all have evil intentions in our heart.

For us to remain humble before the Lord, giving him the credit he is due, I believe we need to understand and practice the fear of God taught in scripture. The kind of fear referred to often in the Old Testament means to stand in awe or reverence. Not necessarily fearful of God as in being scared, but more a fear of his awesome abilities; the destruction he can, and has brought, on arrogant and haughty people.

As a parent, scripture started to make more sense to me. When your children are young they will begin showing their natural rebellious nature, constantly testing you to see how far you will be pushed. It is during the first five to six years of their life that much discipline is needed if you truly desire to teach them obedience.

God's dealings with the Israelites in the first five books of the Bible may seem harsh to some people, until you realize that God was their loving father. He knew he had to discipline them severely in the early stages so that they knew His limits. It can be difficult to understand why so many Israelites had to die by the hand of God, until you remember that God was more concerned about the total body of his people, rather than the interests of a few rebellious people within that body.

What's remarkable is to study the journey of the Israelites, and to see how quickly they forgot God's lessons. I have a Children's Bible storybook that goes through the Bible using one-page stories. I used to read these stories to my daughter when she was five and six years old. As we would read the stories of God's mercy on the Israelites, the very next day we would read how they rebelled. Over and over the same theme was so obvious to my young daughter that she would joke with me "Here they go again Daddy, when will they ever learn." Hopefully we can learn from their lessons and try to be obedient, rather than constantly rebelling.

If you need a good object lesson as to God's mighty power and the reason we should show him respect and reverence try studying Numbers 16. I recently spent some time in this chapter and was amazed at the foolishness of the Israelites. This is the chapter where Korah, Dathan, and Abiram decided that Moses had no right to tell them what God wanted them to do. They gathered 250 people to help them rebel against Moses and Aaron.

The true fear of God was apparent in Moses as he immediately fell facedown on the ground in fear of what God was going to do to these rebellious people. The next morning Moses told everyone to step away from the tents of these three renegades, because God was going to swallow them into the earth. Sure enough right on cue the earth opened up and swallowed them and their family whole without a trace of them to be found. The remaining people ran for their life in fear of what almighty God may do to them.

I would like to think that if I just witnessed God's mighty hand wipe families from the face of the earth that I would think long and hard about challenging God again. Not these stubborn people. The very next day they were at it again. They had the audacity to blame Moses for the loss of their friends, and started the rebellion all over again. Since they obviously didn't learn their lesson God decided to wipe these arrogant people out. A plague swept through their midst and took 14,700 lives before Aaron was able to atone for their sins in the temple, and stop the plague from spreading further.

Now my friends, God does not show us this same kind of judgment today for our rebellious ways, but He is still the same God that is capable of this sort of action. He should be feared and revered in our lives each and every day, whether things are going great or poorly. If you want to continue putting God first in your business, if you want to continue to hang on to a close relationship with God, while hopefully retaining the prosperity that God desires to give us when we are obedient, then please heed His instruction. Humble yourself before God. Show our loving Father the respect, the awe, and the fear He deserves.

Closing

We serve a great God! He is a just God, a loving God, a friend in need, and a wise counselor. He desires for us to know Him intimately, and to follow Him with all our heart. He has given us a guidebook in the Bible that will give us the answers we need in our business if we just spend time in it.

I hope by now you have realized that this book was written not solely for the purpose that you might prosper, although I believe that if you honor your part of God's covenants He will desire to give you that gift, but so that you may experience the fullness of God's love, and his amazing wisdom and knowledge in your business.

I pray you will turn away from the world's solutions to your business problems. Instead you will seek God's counsel both through prayer, His Word, and through His Holy Spirit leading so that you will take the high road every step of the way.

The desire of Integrity Resource Center is that God will receive the glory over the business world in good times and in bad times. We desire to see righteousness prevail by encouraging business people to focus on repentance and obedience to God's commands. We pray that this commitment will be reflected in your lives, your businesses, and will become a testimony to your employees, suppliers, customers, and competitors.

Resource List

Business Resource List

The following is a list of just a few of the ministries to the business community. Each one serves a unique purpose that may assist you in glorifying God through your workplace.

Alliance Defense Fund This is a servant organization that provides the resources that will keep the door open for the spread of the Gospel through the legal defense and advocacy of religious freedom, sanctity of life, and traditional family values. Alliance Defense Fund, 15333 N. Pima Road Suite 165, Scottsdale, AZ 85260, Telephone: (800) TELL-ADF, www.alliancedefensefund.org.

Business Reform Foundation Business Reform magazine is a Christian business magazine circulating to over 100,000 Christian business leaders throughout the world. The mission of Business Reform is to apply God's Word into business. In addition Business Reform has an active website with daily business news and business commentary from a Biblical worldview. For more details go to www.businessreform.com or call 1(866) 6-REFORM.

CBMC Forums A CBMC FORUM is a small group of Christian business owners or leaders who are encouraged to use their business and marketplace as a platform for ministry. A CBMC FORUM can help you affect the lives of employees, suppliers, customers and competitors. CBMC Forum, 2130 East Fourth Street, Suite 125 Santa Ana, CA 92705, Telephone: (714) 543-9500, Fax: (714) 543-9505, www.cbmcforums.com, E-mail: smcreynolds@cbmc.com.

CBMC The mission of CBMC is to present Jesus Christ as Savior and Lord to business and professional men, and to develop Christian business and professional men to carry out the Great Commission. CBMC, 6650 East Brainerd Rd., Suite 100 Chattanooga, TN 37421, Telephone: 423.698.4444 | 1.800.566.CBMC, www.cbmc.com.

CBMC International CBMC International is a worldwide network of business and professional people and organizations seeking to take the truths of Jesus Christ to the marketplace. CBMC International, 3060 Harrodsburg Road, Suite 203, Lexington, KY 40503, Telephone: 859-219-2440, Fax: 859-219-1566, E-mail: cbmcint@cbmcint.org, www.cbmcint.org.

Character That Counts The mission of Character That Counts is to communicate the unique and critical message of character (doing right), integrity (being whole through Christ) and accountability (honestly reporting to one another) into our daily lives. Rod Handley, 1440 SW Jefferson, Lee's Summit MO 64081, Telephone: 816-525-6339, Fax: 816-524-3182, www.characterthatcounts.org.

Christian Legal Society CLS is a national non-denominational membership organization of attorneys, judges, law professors, and law students, working in association with others, to follow Jesus' command "to do justice with the love of God." (Luke 11:42; Matthew 23:23). Christian Legal Society, 4208 Evergreen Lane, Suite 222, Annandale, VA 22003-3264, Telephone: (703) 642-1070, Fax: (703) 642-1075, www.clsnet.org.

Crown Financial Ministries Crown's mission is Teaching People God's Financial Principles. This ministry is primarily focused on personal finances, but it continues to be the catalyst for many business ministries through Larry Burkett's book and seminars on "Business by the Book." Crown Financial Ministries, P.O. Box 100, Gainesville, GA 30503-0100, Telephone: 770-534-1000, www.crown.org.

Executive Ministries (a Campus Crusade ministry) Executive Ministries was established to identify and train Christians to reach and disciple their peers for Christ, and also to provide Staff to assist in the development of a local ministry. Executive Ministries, 201 West McBee Avenue, Suite 201, Greenville, SC 29601, Telephone: (864) 370-3115, Fax: (864) 370-3714, www.execmin.org.

Fellowship of Companies for Christ International "The purpose of the Fellowship of Companies for Christ International is to encourage and equip Christian Chief Executive Officers (CEO's) and Company Owners to operate their businesses and conduct their personal lives according to Biblical principles in pursuit of Christ's eternal objectives." FCCI International Office, P.O. Box 270784, Oklahoma City, OK 73137-0784, Telephone: (800) 664-3224 or (405)-917-1681, Fax: (405) 949-0005, www.fcci.org.

Marketplace Leaders Marketplace Leaders was founded by Os Hillman in 1996 to help men and women identify and fulfill their God-given calling by applying biblical faith to their life and work. Os is also the director of International Coalition of Workplace Ministries. Os Hillman, Marketplace Leaders/Aslan Group Publishing, 3520 Habersham Club Drive, Cumming, GA 30041, Telephone: 678-455-6262, Email: os@marketplaceleaders.org, www.marketplaceleaders.org.

Marketplace Ministries Marketplace Ministries exists to share God's love through chaplains in the workplace by on-site Employee Care Program for client companies. Marketplace Ministries, Inc., 12900 Preston Rd., Suite 1215, Dallas, TX 75230, Telephone: 972-385-7657 or 800-775-7657, mmihq@marketplaceministries.com, www.marketplaceministries.com.

Mockler Center for Faith and Ethics in the Workplace The Colman M. Mockler Center equips the church and its members to bring the work of Christ into the activities of daily life, especially life in the workplace. The Center engages in education, direct ministry, and research to bring the resources of Biblical interpretation, Christian theology and ethics, and practical ministry into the working world. Its mission is carried out in three areas: in the Gordon-Conwell community, in partnership with churches, and directly in the workplace. Mockler Center for Faith and Ethics in the Workplace, Gordon-Conwell Theological Seminary, 130 Essex Street, South Hamilton, MA 01982, Telephone: 978-646-4072, Fax: 978-646-4565, Email: mockler@gcts.edu, www.gordonconwell.edu/ockenga/mockler/index.html

National Christian Foundation The National Christian Foundation exists for a larger purpose: to help Christians advance the Kingdom of God. The principal way we fulfill this purpose is through effective stewardship. Since its founding in 1982, the Foundation has been visionary in identifying ways to make it easier for you to give—and to maximize the impact of your gifts. Over the last 20 years, they have served thousands of believers assisting them in making grants of over $500 million to thousands of charitable organizations. The National Christian Foundation, 1100 Johnson Ferry Road, Suite 900, Atlanta, GA 30342, Telephone: 800-681-6223. www.NationalChristian.com.

Navigators-Business and Professional B&P helps integrate and extend faith into the world. They equip leaders to demonstrate: the love of Christ in their relationships, the justice of Christ in their negotiations, the ethics of Christ in their decisions, the attractiveness of Christ in their person, the focus of Christ in their purpose. Vision statement: Transforming the marketplace, one person at a time. Mission statement: To Know Christ and to make Him known by reaching, discipling and equipping lifelong laborers in the marketplace through successive generations. Business & Professional Ministries 16980 Dallas Parkway, #203, Dallas, TX 75248 Phone: (972) 931-8656, Email: jkennedy@bpnavs.org, www.bpnavigators.org.

Integrity Resource Center, Inc.

Rick Boxx is the President of Integrity Resource Center, Inc., a 501(c)3 nonprofit ministry. The mission of Integrity Resource Center is to impact the marketplace for Christ by practicing, teaching, and promoting God's Word to business leaders.

Our vision is to build a comprehensive biblically based resource center that will connect business leaders with the resources and ministries they need to more effectively impact their workplace for Christ. We desire to be a unifying force between the business community and other ministries that meet the needs of business leaders.

Integrity Resource Center also offers our biblically based "Prosperity Plan," which combines business planning, financial management, and integrity into an ongoing plan for success. Through the "Prosperity Plan" we work one on one with businesses, discipling them each month in the implementation of biblical approaches to business.

We also provide free phone counseling to business and church leaders, teach Crown Financial Ministries "Business by The Book" seminars, speak to groups about biblically based solutions to business and ethical issues, and by sharing biblical insights into business and ethical dilemmas through a weekly Integrity Moments broadcast email.

To contact us write or call Integrity Resource Center, P.O. Box 6112, Leawood, KS 66206-6112, Telephone: (913) 642-8778, Fax: (913) 642-8708, Email: rboxx@IntegrityMoments.com, www.IntegrityMoments.com

To order additional copies of
How To Prosper In Business...
Without Sacrificing Integrity
Or
To receive information about hosting a How To Prosper In

Business Workshop or to have Rick Boxx speak to your group
    Call (800) 355-6071 or email Rick at
    rboxx@IntegrityMoments.com
    Or visit Integrity Resource Center's website at
    www.IntegrityMoments.com.

    Requests can also be mailed to
    Rick Boxx

Integrity Resource Center
PO Box 25301
Overland Park, KS 66225
www.integrityresource.org